Running Events

This is the first book to critically examine the relationship between running events in local, national and international welfare policy, their marketing and management, and the resulting social impacts.

Drawing on original empirical research, the book presents a series of illustrative case studies, with each chapter containing take-home messages for sport and events managers looking to improve their professional practice. Developing a new theoretical perspective on running events, the book presents data from around the world, including five European countries, the US and China. It covers different types of events, from big city marathons to community park runs, and new types of events such as path and trail runs, night runs, ultra runs, extreme runs and obstacle runs, presenting a typology of running events that will help shape the future analysis of this rapidly growing sector. The book also examines the market for running events, runners' socio-demographic profiles, the main management and marketing approaches and techniques used by organisers, and the socio-economic impacts of running events, such as the effect on people's attitudes and behaviours, organisational planning, city promotion and social interactions.

Running events are central to sport at all levels, from grassroots to professional, so this book is essential reading for any student, researcher or practitioner working in sport management, sport development, sport policy, the sociology of sport or event studies.

Kostas Alexandris is a Professor at Aristotle University of Thessaloniki, Greece and an invited faculty member at Sheffield Hallam University, UK. He is also the Director of the "Sport, Tourism and Recreation Management" Lab. He is an Associate Editor in the journals *Managing Sport and Leisure* and *Leisure Studies*, and a member of the editorial boards of several international journals.

Vassil Girginov is a Professor in sport management/development at Brunel University London, UK, and a Visiting Professor at the Russian International Olympic University, Russia and the University of Johannesburg, South Africa. He also serves as the President of the European Association for Sport Management. His work is concerned with understanding the relationship between the Olympic Games and social change in various cultural and economic milieus. His research interests, publications and industry experience are in the field of Olympic movement, sport development, comparative management and policy analysis.

Jeroen Scheerder is a Professor in sport policy and sport sociology in the Department of Movement Sciences, KU Leuven, Belgium, where he heads the Policy in Sports & Physical Activity Research Group. He is the promotor-coordinator of the Interuniversity Policy Research Centre on Sports on behalf of the Flemish Government, and the academic coordinator of the KU Leuven Sport Policy & Sport Management Programme. He also served as the President of the European Association for Sociology of Sport (2014–2016). He is (co-)editor of *Running across Europe* (2015), *Functions of Sports Clubs in European Societies* (2020), and *The Rise and Size of the Fitness Industry in Europe* (2020).

European Association for Sport Management Series
Series Editors
Guillaume Bodet, Claude Bernard University Lyon 1, France
Tracy Taylor, Victoria University, Australia

Consistent with the aims of the European Association of Sport Management (EASM), the objectives of the EASM book series are to contribute to the dissemination of scholarly knowledge of sport management practices in Europe, support applied investigations and intellectual enquiry into sport management within a European context, and provide readers with new insights, innovations and challenges associated with sport management.

Available in this series:

Running Events
Policies, Marketing and Impacts
Kostas Alexandris, Vassil Girginov and Jeroen Scheerder

For more information about this series, please visit: http://www.routledge.com/ European-Association-of-Sport-Management-Series/book-series/EASM

Running Events
Policies, Marketing and Impacts

Kostas Alexandris, Vassil Girginov and
Jeroen Scheerder

LONDON AND NEW YORK

First published 2023
by Routledge
4 Park Square, Milton Park, Abingdon, Oxon OX14 4RN

and by Routledge
605 Third Avenue, New York, NY 10158

Routledge is an imprint of the Taylor & Francis Group, an informa business

© 2023 Kostas Alexandris, Vassil Girginov and Jeroen Scheerder

The right of Kostas Alexandris, Vassil Girginov and Jeroen Scheerder to be identified as authors of this work has been asserted in accordance with sections 77 and 78 of the Copyright, Designs and Patents Act 1988.

All rights reserved. No part of this book may be reprinted or reproduced or utilised in any form or by any electronic, mechanical, or other means, now known or hereafter invented, including photocopying and recording, or in any information storage or retrieval system, without permission in writing from the publishers.

Trademark notice: Product or corporate names may be trademarks or registered trademarks, and are used only for identification and explanation without intent to infringe.

British Library Cataloguing-in-Publication Data
A catalogue record for this book is available from the British Library

Library of Congress Cataloging-in-Publication Data
Names: Alexandris, Kostas, author. | Girginov, Vassil, 1956– author. | Scheerder, Jeroen, author.
Title: Running events : policies, marketing and impacts / Kostas Alexandris, Vassil Girginov and Jeroen Scheerder.
Description: Abingdon, Oxon ; New York, N.Y. : Routledge, 2023. | Series: European association of sport management series | Includes bibliographical references and index. |
Identifiers: LCCN 2022046518 | ISBN 9781032294599 (hardback) | ISBN 9781032294629 (paperback) | ISBN 9781003301691 (ebook)
Subjects: LCSH: Running races—Management. | Running races—Marketing. | Running races—Social aspects. | Sports administration. | Hosting of sporting events.
Classification: LCC GV713 .A48 2023 | DDC 796.4206/9—dc23/eng/20221013
LC record available at https://lccn.loc.gov/2022046518

ISBN: 978-1-032-29459-9 (hbk)
ISBN: 978-1-032-29462-9 (pbk)
ISBN: 978-1-003-30169-1 (ebk)

DOI: 10.4324/9781003301691

Typeset in Times New Roman
by codeMantra

Contents

List of figures	xi
List of tables	xiii
List of contributors	xv
Foreword	xvii
SEBASTIAN COE	
Acknowledgements	xix
List of abbreviations	xxi

1 **The many facets of running**   1
VASSIL GIRGINOV

Running events 4
Running studies 5
Plan of this book 10

2 **The running eventscape: Developments, runners' profiles and policies**   18
JEROEN SCHEERDER AND KOBE HELSEN

Introduction 18
Developments in the running industry 20
    Three waves of running 20
    Running waves in numbers 26
Runners' profiles 31
    Demographics 31
    Motives for running 32
    Social status 34
Policy actors in the running market 36
    Role of running providers 36
    Role of the public sector 39
    Public value and the need for collaboration 40
Conclusions 41

Case study 2.1 The AG Antwerp Ten Miles & Marathon and the Brussels 20 km Race Trends in Participant Numbers and Profiles 50
Case study 2.2 The AG Antwerp Ten Miles & Marathon and the Eindejaarscorrida Leuven Comparing Events Policy, Events Marketing and Events Impact Between a Commercial and Voluntary Running Event Provider 58

3 **Marketing running events** 65
KOSTAS ALEXANDRIS, PAUL HOVER, AND LINDA OOMS

The product of running events 66
Marketing implications 68
   Concentrate on a type of impact and target audience 68
   Co-create the running event concept 68
   Organise auxiliary activities 69
   Support the core product with appropriate services from the destination in which the event takes place 70
The place and time of running events 71
Marketing implications 72
   Choose an event location that is easily accessible by public or active transportation 72
   Choose an event location that offers possibilities to add additional local services 72
The promotion of running events 72
Market segmentation 73
Marketing implications 76
   Invest enough time and resources in getting to know the target audience 76
Branding of running events 76
Marketing implications 79
   Develop a distinctive and appropriate running event concept 79
Communication strategy 79
Marketing implications 82

Promote the running event in a way
that is appealing to the target audience 82
Conclusions 82
Case study 3.1 Marathon Amersfoort,
The Netherlands 86
Case study 3.2 Athens Marathon: The authentic 92

4 **Running events' impacts** 98
VASSIL GIRGINOV

Running events impacts: taking stock of
current knowledge 99
Visions of impact 104
Delivering running events impacts 107
Case study 4.1 The LifeSouth race
weekend, Gainesville, Florida 117
Case study 4.2 Running events in China
and their impact 123

5 **Conclusion** 132
VASSIL GIRGINOV

Introduction 132
From Couch to 5k: the politics, marketing
and impact of running events 133
Studying running events 137
Running events and sustainable development 138

Index 141

Figures

2.1	Number of marathon events and finishers, worldwide data (1960–2015)	26
2.2	Number of marathon events with more than 1,000 finishers and number of finishers at 20 largest marathons, worldwide data (1960–2015)	27
2.3	Number of finishers at the 100 largest road races in the US (2001–2019)	28
2.4	Number of running events and finishers in Japan (2009–2018)	29
2.5	Number of running events, finishers and runners in Flanders, Belgium (1969–2019)	30
2.6	Evolution of male/female ratios for marathon participation in different countries (1970–2015)	32
2.7	Social status pyramid of sports participation in Flanders, Belgium, according to socio-professional status	35
2.8	Multi-sector model for the organisation and provision of recreational running	37
2.9	Number of finishers at the AG Antwerp Ten Miles & Marathon and the Brussels 20 km race (1980–2022)	51
2.10	Number of finishers at the AG Antwerp Ten Miles & Marathon, according to different distances that were offered (2003–2022)	52
2.11	Evolution of finishing times at the Brussels 20 km race (1988–2018)	55
2.12	Evolution of finishing times at the AG Antwerp Ten Miles & Marathon (1988–2018)	55
3.1	Educational level of runners by race	94
3.2	Average age of runners by race	94
3.3	Gender of runners by race	95
4.1	Number of running events in China	123

Tables

1.1	A typology of running events	10
1.2	Key characteristics of studied running events	12
2.1	Different waves in the development of post-WWII recreational running	25
2.2	Continental marathon market shares in 1980, 2000 and 2015, in percentages	30
2.3	Evolution of the number of female finishers at the Brussels 20 km race (1984–2022), in percentages	53
2.4	Average age of finishers at two popular Flemish running events (between 2010 and 2019)	53
4.1	Impact types of running events	100
4.2	Definitions of sociocultural impacts	101
4.3	Relationship between selected running events' goals, public support and impacts	106
4.4	Running events resources	108

Contributors

Panagiota Balaska is an Adjunct Lecturer at Open University, Greece and a Research Assistant in the "Sport, Tourism and Leisure Management" Lab (AUTH). Her research interest is in the area of event management.

Kobe Helsen is a Research Assistant for the Policy in Sports & Physical Activity Research Group, at KU Leuven, Belgium.

Paul Hover is a Senior Researcher at the Mulier Institute, The Netherlands. His research focuses on sports marketing, sports economics and sports management. He is also an advisor of the Dutch Sports Council and a member of the advisory committee of the Brabant Sport Fund.

Kyriaki (Kiki) Kaplanidou is a Professor in the Department of Sport Management at the University of Florida, USA.

Thomas Karagiorgos is an Adjunct Lecturer at Open University, Greece and a Research Assistant in the "Sport, Tourism and Leisure Management" Lab (AUTH). He is an outdoor professional, with a research focus on outdoor recreation management.

Yue Liu is the Deputy General Manager of Wanda Sports and a Member of the Road Race Commission of the Chinese Athletic Association, China.

Apostolia Ntovoli is a Lecturer at Frederick University, Cyprus and a Research Assistant in the "Sport, Tourism and Leisure Management" Lab (AUTH). Her research interest is in the area of sport marketing.

Linda Ooms is a Researcher in the field of sports, physical activity and health. Working at the Mulier Institute, The Netherlands, she focuses her projects in facilitating physical activity levels among less physically active people. In addition, she focuses on the theoretical groundwork, monitoring and evaluation of sport and physical activity interventions for specific target groups and the mental effects of sport and physical activity participation.

Xiaoyan Xing is a Professor in the School of Sport Management and Communications at the Capital University of Physical Education and Sports, Beijing Institute for International Olympic Studies, China.

Foreword

Sebastian Coe

I have been a runner my whole life. I can't remember a time when I did not run, nor a time when I did not love running. I have run for a living, run recreationally, organised running events, promoted and commentated on them and now head up the International Governing body that certifies, regulates and creates running partnerships in all its forms.

I have read many books on running but, to my knowledge, none come close to pulling together such an eclectic and thorough body of research from around the world – historic and present – and so thoughtfully lays it out to create a forensic study of the history and development of running.

I am a passionate believer in history and have always believed that by understanding the history of the sport you participate in at an elite level, club level or recreational level, it will help you be better at it and enjoy it more. I also believe that reading and understanding history help us all make better decisions in the future. And this book does just this. It clearly and simply reviews why people run and why governments, through the decades, have supported running and shines a light on the opportunity to increase running for the benefit of all.

I am often told that running is a solitary occupation and, for some, this is true. But running is one of the few sports that can be both solitary and sociable. Over 4bn people around the world run regularly and millions more take part in organised running events. And it is running events that this book illuminates the most. Highlighting the importance of governments, event organisers, businesses and participants to come together to deliver. It is a sport that benefits and grows from co-partnering, where each partner is entirely reliant on the others to create the event, promote the event, host the event and participate in it. Every partner has a leading role – particularly those that participate in running events. As this book points out, they are co-producers of the event. Without them, there can be no event.

That running has been a core part of government health and wellbeing agendas for decades comes as no surprise to me, but what this book has made me think more about is why, through all the efforts of government, business and sport, have we not quite managed to fully democratise running. It is still weighted to those in higher socioeconomic groups. I can't help believe that this may also link to another observation in the book that so few of the hundreds of thousands of running events around the world conduct any type of impact study – other than participant numbers, reach of social media and possibly television. If we undertook more impact studies of these events, and this book goes into some detail of what these studies might look like, then perhaps we will understand more about the inherent barriers to running and work on making this a sport or an activity that appeals to all.

Running is both tangible and intangible but as the book quotes, "we should no longer merely be trying to run 'sustainable events'; rather, we should focus on how events can contribute to the sustainable economic, social and environmental development of the places which host them" and if I may be so bold as to add … "and to the people, the co-producers, who run in them and who have yet to run in them".

Sebastian Coe
President, World Athletics
September 2022
Monaco

Acknowledgements

The authors would like to thank the partners of the "Promoting health enhancing physical activity and social-welfare through outdoor running events / RUN for HEALTH" Erasmus+ sport programme: Aristotle University of Thessaloniki (Kostas Alexandris, George Grouios, Vassilis Barkoukis, Thomas Karagiorgos, Apostolia Ntovoli, Despina Ourda, George Bouchouras), Breda University of Applied Sciences (Marisa de Brito, Anne-Marie Geijsel, Ellis Middelkamp, Lorraine van Liere, Ondrej Mitas), Brunel University (Vassil Girginov), EASM (Aila Ahonen, Frau Sara Runzheimer), ECOS (Alessandro Ruggeri, Valerio Di Tomasso and Stefano Moliterni), KU Leuven (Jeroen Scheerder, Kobe Helsen), LSU (Irena Valentine, Edvinas Eimontas, Kristina Mejeryte Narkeviciene, Rasa Kreivyte) and Mulier Institute (Paul Hover, Linda Ooms, Peter van Eldert) for their expertise and valuable insights that made this project possible.

Our appreciative thanks are also extended to Guillaume Bodet and Tracy Taylor, editors of EASM's sport management book series, as well as to Simon Whitmore and Rebecca Connor from Routledge for their belief in and encouragement of this project. The empirical part of the study would not have been possible without the support of event organisers in Belgium, Greece, Italy, Lithuania and The Netherlands. We owe you a great deal of gratitude.

Abbreviations

AAU	American Athletic Union
AIMDR	Association of International Marathons and Distance Races
AIMS	Association of International Marathons
AMA	American Marketing Association
ARSS	Association of Road Racing Statisticians
CAA	Chinese Athletic Association
COP	Conference of the Parties (COP)
DCLA	Daring Club Leuven Atletiek
EKAB	National Centre of Immediate Help
EMBOK	Event Management Body of Knowledge, http://www.embok.org/index.php
ERT	Hellenic Radio and TV
FA	Cup Football Association (FA)
GAS	General Administration of Sport
GER	The Great Ethiopian Run (Addis Ababa, Ethiopia)
GNR	Great North Run (Newcastle, England)
GSC	Gainesville Sports Commission
IAAF	International Amateur Athletic Federation, renamed in 2019 as World Athletics (WA)
MPREs	Mass Participation Running Events
NHS	National Health Service
NYM	New York Marathon
OASA	Association of Transport of Athens
OPAP	Organisation for Football Prognostics
R4H	Run for Health
SDGs	Sustainable Development Goals
SEGAS	Hellenic Association of Amateur Athletics, http://www.segas.gr
UN	United Nations

WA	World Athletics, previously International Amateur Athletic Federation (IAAF)
WMM	World Marathon Majors (i.e., Tokyo Marathon, Boston Marathon, London Marathon, Berlin Marathon, Chicago Marathon and New York City Marathon)

1 The many facets of running

Vassil Girginov

Running is inherent within human ability and is a complex and coordinated process which involves the entire body. Running has been associated with the earliest forms of human civilisation and both mirror and model social development. Kamphorst and Roberts' (1989) multinational study on sport participation concluded that regardless of context and fads, running has always been a popular activity which is fundamental to human survival and well-being. In the primitive forms of human civilisation, it played a transformative role by enabling hunted people to become hunters. Modern-day running also serves many transformative functions, including enhancing cognitive, social, political, personal and national identity building, stimulating social cohesion, health and entertainment.

Running has not only a functional role but a symbolic one as well. Evidence suggests that ancient Egyptians used running as a *symbol* as early as 3100 BC in the Sed festival celebrating the pharaoh's continued rule. The ruler would need to perform four running ceremonies on a course constructed to represent the lands of Egypt to demonstrate his returned vigour and thus ensure continued prosperity for the country (Uphill, 1965). Thus, running provides the symbolic link between personal fitness, leadership and societal well-being. Running events come from cultural and religious traditions; thus, they mirror the existing social order. Equally, they can also be invented in response to current or projected socio-economic conjunctures, so they model the social order.

Running is multimodal. It can be free, spontaneous, and highly regimental and organised. It can be ritualistic, recreational, competitive, aerobic and anaerobic, cause-related, occupational or necessitated. Running is constantly evolving as well as it assumes new forms, appears in previously unknown spaces and in combination with technology and other forms of exercise. Running classifications abound and employ various criteria, including distance, time, space, season,

DOI: 10.4324/9781003301691-1

access, level of ability and organisation (i.e., local, national or international), among others. For example, at present, World Athletics (previously IAAF – International Amateur Athletics Federation), the international governing body of running, encompasses track and field, road running, race walking, cross-country, mountain and trail running. Many other forms of running exist such as city runs, urban trails, fell running, parkour, run-ups, rural, beach and ultramarathons, most of which are highly organised and internationally governed. Whatever its form, "running exists as an entity, that is, as a recognizable social practice thanks to the different ways of practicing or performing that a runner continuously develops in a given territorial and historical context" (Capsi & LLopis-Goig, 2021, p. 6).

Running is purposeful. Various modes of running are closely related to the motivation of participants. Understanding runners' motivation is critical for making sense of the 'running world' and its relationship with society and is largely premised on the theoretical perspective employed. Eichberg (1998) proposed a trialectical anthropological model of reasons for running, including for fun, fitness and for achievement, which was largely confirmed by Malchrowicz and Poczta's (2018) four basic types of orientation of runners, including social, experience, factual and result-driven. Llopis-Going and Llopis-Going's (2012) sociocultural classification model identifies four ideal types of runners, including lone hedonists, competitive individualists, sociable runners and disciplined group members. Using demographic, psychographic as well as behavioural characteristics, and a sample of over 7,100 runners, Vos and Scheerder (2009) identified five types of runners in the Flemish running market, namely: (i) individual runners (41%), (ii) social competitive runners (26%), (iii) companionship runners (18%), (iv) fitness runners (9%) and (v) individual competitive runners (7%). This typology is in line with the ones presented by, among others, Delnoij (2004) and Rohm et al. (2006). A recent systematic review of psychological and behavioural correlates of recreational running examined 58 studies and reported that the highest-ranked motives were physical health, psychological motives and personal achievement (Pereira et al, 2021).

Marketing prefers different categories which are typically derived from extensive research, and which serve specific organisational objectives. For example, in 2016, England Athletics developed a National Running Tracker designed to generate insights to help understand the factors determining runners' participation, which currently includes a sample of over 35,000 runners. The Tracker segments the English-running market into six categories, including connected challengers (14%), active escapists (21%), balance boosters (13%), reassurance reachers (17%), hesitant aspires (17%) and independent casuals (20%) (England Athletics, n.d.). Whatever the theoretical perspective on runners' motivation, knowledge about it helps shape their experiences and organisational practices.

Running is contested. Whatever its form, running always takes place in a particular historical context and has been the subject of contested interpretations. The current popularity of mass running only started to emerge in the USA and thereafter in Europe in the 1970s and 1980s. Prior to that, running was largely associated in public consciousness with uniformity, centralisation and bureaucratisation of the stadium track, so the open running boom was also a reaction against what Bale (2004) has called the 'Fordism' of track running. Yet, the premier US running event, the Boston Marathon, only started to admit women after 1972. The expansion of running has also come with health, economic and environmental costs. Hespanhol Junior et al. (2016) found that 33% of 161 runners they studied suffered an injury which represented significant economic burden for public health (€57.97 on average because of healthcare expenses and indirect costs caused by missing work because of the injuries of €115.75). Sleeswijk et al. (2021) document similar results (€74 per running injury and €35 per participant). Global running statistics reports a 65% increase in running and jogging activities in 2020, but at the same time about 37–70% of competitive and recreational runners get injured yearly. Between 50 and 70% of running injuries are caused by overuse (Rizzo, 2021), which is an indication of runners' over-commitment.

Dr Kenneth Cooper, the author of the popular Cooper fitness test, has opined that anyone running more than 15 minutes a day was running for reasons other than health (Plymire, 2004). Running has always had its advocates and sceptics. In the *Non-Runner's Book*, Ziegel and Grossberger (1978, pseudonyms of two successful Sneaker manufacturers) provided a practical guide with recommendations for those who want to drop out of the faddish rat race called running. Ziegel and Grossberger's ironic book can be considered as a confirmation of the popularity of mass running. Committed running has created the addicted runner, and thus has opened the possibility for the systematic organisation and control of bodies or the exercise of what Foucault (1979) has termed 'biopower' and 'biopolitics'. These processes involve the collection of information through surveillance which recently has become readily available with the advent of wearable technologies and the dissemination of knowledge with the purposes of producing docile bodies.

Running is manufactured. Bale (2004, p. 1) writes that "after walking, running is the first technology of the body that, through human agency seeks to compress time and space". The present book is concerned with manufactured running, that is, the policies, structures, practices, the organisation of space, participants and resources needed for staging running events as well as their leveraging and tangible and intangible impacts. While anyone can put on their running shoes and go for a jog in the park or along the streets, bringing together a group of people in one place for the same run requires significant amount of work, strategic and operational decision making and resources. The manufacturing of running is a complex and systematic process (Garcia-Vallejo et al., 2020), which has been aided greatly by the two concurrent processes of standardisation and commercialisation.

Both standardisation and commercialisation of running have proceeded steadily over time, from the earliest running event on record held in Ireland in 1896 BC in honour of the Irish goddess and queen Aonach Tailtiu (Cronin, 2003), to the first purpose-built running track in England in 1837, the introduction of the starting blocks in Chicago in 1929, and qualification norms, control of equipment and doping testing and the prize money, television rights and commercial sponsorship (Krieger, 2021).

Running events' standardisation has led to an enhanced level of control over athletes, event organisers and spectators' behaviour as well as over the impact of those events. For example, the *European Athletics Quality Road Race Standards* act as an assurance for road runners throughout Europe and includes three levels of standards encompassing all types and sizes of races (i.e., 1, 3 and 5 stars, https://www.european-running4all.org/en/standards/). The setting of standards involves an elaborate governance process of consultations with runners, race organisers, European Athletics Member Federations and competition and medical experts as well as an institutional framework to ensure their legitimacy and credibility.

Running became formally institutionalised internationally in 1912 at the Stockholm Olympic Games in Sweden when delegates from 17 national athletics federations met and founded the International Amateur Athletic Federation (IAAF, renamed in 2019 as World Athletics) as the world governing body for the sport of track and field athletics. In 2022, World Athletics boasts 214 national member federations, which is every country in the world, and which also exceeds the number of United Nations (UN) member states that officially stands at 193.

Running events

If running is a technology of the body that, through human agency seeks to compress time and space, as Bale (2004) argues, running events connect the event where the compression takes place to the wider world beyond it. Here, Handelman (1998) offers a powerful explanation: "Public events are locations of communication that convey participants into versions of social order in relatively coherent ways" (p. 15). He further contends that the mandate of public events

> is to engage in the ordering of ideas, people and things. As phenomena, they not only are cognitively graspable but emotionally livable. Therefore, they are devices of praxis that merge horizons of the ideal and the real, to bring into close conjunction ideology and practice, attitude and action.
>
> (p. 16)

Handelman (1998) also makes clear that the activation of a public event is contingent on the practice of its logic of its organisational design. This understanding brings together into a coherent whole the symbolism, institutional design and the practices of running events. From a social practice theory point of view, practices are interdependent relationships of materials, meaning and competencies (Shove et al., 2012). In the contest of running, materials involve equipment, technology (i.e., hand watches and mobile telephones), services and space. Meaning concerns motivations, emotions and the symbolic aspects of the event. Competencies of practice relate to the skills and knowledge needed to identify as a runner, to appreciate and communicate this practice. For Handelman (1998), there are two main forms of public events, including models and mirrors. The former, or events that model, are not mere representations of social order; rather, they are creating social order. The latter are public events that represent social order. Regardless of their form, public events are symbolic structures that possess relational qualities between presence and absence where symbolism plays a critical role: "A symbol stands for, evokes or brings into being something else, something absent" (p. 13). The approach to running events employed in this book discusses both categories and their relationships with politics, marketing and impacts. This is a challenging undertaking since running events have increasingly been viewed by governments and other agencies as 'lifestyle medicine' (Filo & Coghan, 2016). Labelling running events as a universal solution to societal ills runs the risk of undermining their authenticity and prioritising instrumental over intrinsic purposes.

Running studies

In answering the question 'why study public events', Handelman (1998) argues that "events are important phenomena because they constitute a dense concentration of symbols and their associations are of relevance to particular people" (p. 9). Handelman was speaking from an anthropological perspective on events, but despite their appeal to people and societies, as Bale (2004, p. 1) noted, "as a body-cultural phenomenon running has eluded serious study in the humanities and social sciences". This is not to deny the voluminous body of literature on various aspects of running, including history, arts, statistical guides and biographies of runners. Several recent systematic reviews help to grasp the scope of running studies ranging from running injuries (Kakouris et al., 2021; van der Worp et al., 2015), to the effects of training periodisation (Casado & Santos-Concejero, 2017; Kenneally et al., 2017), mindfulness (Corbally et al., 2020), growth of running (Scheerder et al., 2015), effects of footwear (Cheung & Ngai, 2016) and running technology (Seuter et al., 2017).

More broadly, Getz (2012) has made the first systematic attempt to document the emergence of a field of enquiry dedicated to event studies. Mair and Whitford's (2013) review of events research reveals that the areas of definitions and types of events, and events logistics and staging have been comprehensively researched and that further research is unlikely to yield any new knowledge. They also suggest that future events research needs to explore the socio-cultural and environmental impacts of events along with a better understanding of the relationship between events and public policy agendas. The current book tries to answer this call.

Andrews and Leopold (2013) developed a rare comprehensive social sciences perspective on events studies by anchoring them in society and the interactions between people and places which produce event impacts. The authors identified three main features of the study of events, including *place* (i.e., boundaries and access; sense of place and belonging; architecture, urban design, landscape and transformation, commodification of place displacement, politics); *business* (i.e., management, marketing, planning and development resources, public relations and commerce); and *socio-cultural* (i.e., identity habitus people: psychological and physiological needs, experiences and meanings; the body and gender) (p. 3). The three features of event studies suggest that running events' policies, marketing and impacts are closely interrelated and need to be studied holistically.

The systematic study of events has also resulted in further codifying this knowledge domain through the development of various tools and online platforms. *The Event Management Body of Knowledge* (EMBOK, http://www.embok.org/index.php) platform was set up with the explicit aim to promote research and knowledge generation and dissemination in the field. Similar online platforms were established elsewhere, and they serve as an important reference point for researchers, participants and event promoters (e.g., the UK, http://www.eventimpacts.com/).

Since this book explores the relationship between running events and their policies, promotion and impacts, and given the huge variety of forms and types of running, it makes sense to establish a typology to guide the analysis. Admittedly, it would have been perfectly reasonable for such a typology to emerge at the end of the book as well, but the authors decided to take a deductive approach and to place it in the introduction, so it can serve as a heuristic device and guide the reader. As far as can be ascertained, no agreed upon running events typology exist apart from governing bodies' own classifications of running based on distances, participants ages and spaces where running takes place.

Typologies represent organised systems of types and are a well-established tool in social sciences. Their main purpose is to assist in forming and refining concepts, drawing out underlying dimensions, creating categories for classification and measurement, and sorting cases (Collier et al., 2012). Collier et al. (2012) distinguish between conceptual typologies, descriptive vs explanatory and multidimensional vs unidimensional typologies. Our aim is to develop a conceptual typology of running events. The main function of this type of typology is to explicate the meaning of a concept by mapping out its dimensions. In this way, it becomes possible for the analysis to relate policies, marketing and impacts to different types of running events and to outline how their dimensions shape certain actions, experiences and outcomes.

Running events represent special public occurrences that take place in a given time and space. These are planned events, that is, they have well-defined purposes, target groups, format, governance arrangements, and which have certain kinds of public appeal and impact. Therefore, by definition, running events are social constructs, and, as Jago and Shaw (1998, p. 29) note, they provide participants with a leisure and social opportunity beyond everyday experience. As established in the previous section, as a public event, running events are based on a consequential logic – by showcasing human excellence on the road or the track, they aspire to affect social life by inspiring people to take up sport, to appreciate other cultures, religions and gender and, more broadly, to bring about change by shaping social reality. As Handelman (1998) points out, this is a functional relationship that "lies at the epistemological core of any conception of public event. The features of the public event indicate that it points beyond itself, or in other words, it is symbolic of something outside itself" (p. 12).

The symbolic meaning of running events varies significantly across contexts and cultures, but to affect a positive personal or social change they need to meet some basic human needs. Those needs are captured by the concept of the 'triple bottom line', which focuses on the integration of social well-being, environmental protection and economic viability goals (Fredline et al., 2004). Rogers and Ryan's (2001) discussion of the 'triple bottom line' concept explicates that there are nine basic, universal, human needs, including the need for sustenance, protection, affection, idleness, creativity, freedom, understanding, participation and identity. Furthermore, as both Getz (2012) and Parent and Smith-Swan (2012) point out, the study of sport events has been the subject matter of several academic disciplines, such as anthropology, geography, economics, sociology, management science, history, political science and psychology. Therefore, a discipline-specific perspective will offer different interpretations of the satisfaction of human needs.

At the event-generic level, Getz (2012, p. 41) proposed a typology of planned events, including (i) cultural celebrations, (ii) business and trade, (iii) arts and entertainment, (iv) sport and recreation, (v) political and state, and (vi) private functions. Getz further categorised sporting events into league play/championships, one-off meets/tours, fun events and sport festivals. This typology seems to be rather broad and not analytically helpful. However, Getz explicitly noted the multifaceted functions performed by events, which represents an important dimension in their understanding.

One of the earlier sport events typologies was proposed by Gratton et al. (2000, p. 26), and includes four types of major events according to their economic impact where the word 'major' in each category signifies the importance of sporting outcomes of such events. These include four types:

A: irregular, one-off, major international spectator events generating significant economic activity and media interest (e.g., Olympics, Football World Cup and European Football Championship);
B: major spectator events, generating significant economic activity, media interest and part of an annual domestic cycle of sports events (e.g., FA Cup Final, Six Nations Rugby Union Internationals, Test Match Cricket, Open Golf and Wimbledon);
C: irregular, one-off, major international spectator/competitor events generating limited economic activity (e.g., European Junior

The many facets of running 9

Boxing Championships, European Junior Swimming Championships, World Badminton Championships and IAAF Grand Prix); D: major competitor events generating limited economic activity and are part of an annual cycle of sports events (e.g., National Championships in most sports).

A similar typology for the purposes of bidding and managing events was proposed by UK Sport, which classifies the sporting calendar into four groups within the overall umbrella of major events, including mega, calendar, one-off and showcase events. Here, mega events are awarded after competitive bidding, calendar events require no bidding, one-off events are generally awarded after competitive bidding and generate substantial television rights and interest nationally and internationally, and showcase events which are generally awarded after competitive bidding and have the potential to boost sport development, and improve a country's image (Bowdin et al., 2006).

Building on Jago and Shaw (1998) and Getz (2005), Parent and Smith-Swan (2012) provide a typology of sports events with seven types, including special events (planned); minor sports events (local/community level with relatively low attendance or media attention); festivals (community-based); major sports events (high attendance, media attention); hallmark events (recurring; tied to a place); large-scale sports events (one-off or recurring); and mega sports events (one-off). Despite its level of detail, this typology revolves around one dimension of events, namely their size.

The above typologies outline five important dimensions pertinent to running events, including their ownership, scale, the process of obtaining the right to organise them, formal evaluation and impacts. These five dimensions directly affect the outcomes of any event as they impact on the process of its planning and delivery and regulate the public access to and perception of it. The synthesis of extant events typologies has allowed to establish a typology of running events, which is presented in Table 1.1. The proposed running event typology includes 12 dimensions which in combination allow to grasp the nature of the event and its relationship to either the existing (i.e., mirror) or the emerging social order (i.e., model). This distinction is critical to understand the policies behind running events and how these are promoted and impact people and places.

There is also a significant body of literature on the impact and legacy of sporting events, which is discussed in Chapter 4 of this book. However, literature on running events' impact is sparse but two current systematic reviews of the broader field are worth noting, including

Table 1.1 A typology of running events

Event dimension	Proxy variable	Type
Ownership	Public/private/voluntary organisation	Public/Private/Charity/Partnership
Organiser	Owing organisation/consortium/event company	Owner/Event company
Certification	WA/Europe Athletics/National Federation/other	Certified/Non-certified
Form (mirror or model)	Mass participation; commemorative, regular, for certain type of runners, cause-related; corporate	Mass/competitive/heritage/cause-related
Access	Registration/fee required/free	Inclusive/Exclusive
Function	Stated aims (competitive/charitable/promotional) and outcome (improved well-being/health/participation/awareness/standards/qualifications)	Promoting sport/achievement/health/city/entertainment
Level	Local/national/international	Local/national/international
Location	City streets, park, other	Nature/city
Frequency	Seasonal/regular/irregular	Seasonal/regular/irregular
Participants	Young people, semi/pro athletes	Age/level of running-specific/Open
Funding	Public/commercial/self-funded	Public/commercial/self-funded
Auxiliary/Side activities	Workshops, exhibitions, master classes, public celebrations, research	Stand-alone/auxiliary

Scheu and Preuss (2018) and Koeningstorfer et al. (2017). Both reviews have established the link between events' vision and actual impacts and legacies. Thus, to understand the impact of running events, we need to attend to the visions of events' promoters, the context and format, and how these visions have been carried out to deliver their stated impacts.

Plan of this book

This book grew out of an ERASMUS+-funded project called 'Run for Health' (R4H) which afforded the authors the opportunity to work together along with several other colleagues from Belgium (KU Leuven),

Greece (Aristotle University of Thessaloniki), Finland (JAMK), Lithuania (Lithuanian Sports University), Italy (European Culture & Sport Organization), The Netherlands (Mulier Institute and Breda University of Applied Sciences), the UK (Brunel University London) and the European Association of Sport Management (EASM). Some of the data used in the book are generated by the R4H project, but additional research has also been undertaken to complement existing information. More precisely, the R4H project collected data from 12 running events held in the five countries previously mentioned. Table 1.2 shows the main characteristics of those events. The sample of running events clearly demonstrates that they are of different types and have a varied potential to attract resources and participants, implying that their impacts are very different as well. Since the project's data is from Europe, we wanted to expand the socio-cultural and socio-economic contexts of running and therefore included two case studies from China and the USA written by Xiaoyan Xing and Yue Liu, and Kiriaki Kiplianidou, respectively.

As already noted, this book is structured around three core themes and follows a deductive logic where each main issue is illustrated with two case studies drawn from different contexts. The first theme concerns running events' evolution and policies (Chapter 2). Policies are grounded in values and ideologies and represent visions about some desired end state and the 'how', or the tools used to achieve those visions. Thus, under this heading, the chapter critically analyses the growth of running events and different policies promoted by various actors, the main beneficiaries and their motivations. Two case studies of The AG Antwerp Ten Miles & Marathon and the Brussels 20 km race and The AG Antwerp Ten Miles & Marathon and the Eindejaarscorrida Leuven by Kobe Helsen and Jeroen Scheerder illustrate both trends in running and the role of public policies.

The second theme (Chapter 3) examines aspects of running events marketing and offers an in-depth look into the segmentation, branding and communication strategies of event organisers in achieving the policies discussed in Chapter 2. This chapter engages with the conceptual aspects of events marketing and its practical application. It is supported by two case studies, the first one written by Paul Hover and Linda Ooms about the Marathon Amersfoort in The Netherlands, and the second one written by Karagiorgos, Ntovoli, Balaska and Alexandris about The Athens Authentic Marathon, which illustrate the conceptual aspects presented in the chapter.

The third main theme of the book analyses the impacts of running events (Chapter 4). Those impacts are first articulated in various policies

Table 1.2 Key characteristics of studied running events

Country	Event/Year established	Owner	Organiser	Form	Type/Location	Participants (No)
Belgium	Corrida Leuven 1997	Eindejaarscorrida Leuven	Daring Club Leuven Atletiek vzw (non-profit organisation)	Regular, competitive, mass participation	Heritage/city	6,000
	AG Antwerp 10 miles & Marathon 1986	Golazo Sports	Golazo Sports (private company)	Regular, competitive, mass participation	Competitive/city	29,230
	Bosland Trail 2018	BoslandTrail vzw	Bosland Trail vzw (non-profit organisation)	Regular, competitive	Ecology/nature	3–5,000
Greece	Alexander the Great Intern marathon 2006	Triton Sport Club	Triton Sport Club	Regular, competitive, mass participation	Recreational/ Competitive/city	20,000
	The Athens Authentic marathon 1972	The Hellenic Association of Amateur Athletics (SEGAS)	The Hellenic Association of Amateur Athletics (SEGAS)	Regular, competitive, mass participation	Recreational/ Competitive/ city	50,000

Country	Event	Organiser	Type of participation	Competition type	Participants
Italy	Chiavari 2014		Local authorities	Regular, competitive, mass participation	Competitive & recreational/city	1,200
	Ravenna marathon 2011	Ravena Runners Club	Runners club	Regular, competitive, mass participation	Heritage Competitive/city	18,000
	Florence marathon 1984			Regular, competitive, mass participation	Competitive & recreational/city	9,000
Lithuania	Bristonas half marathon 2016	Asociacija 'Savas miestas'/ Association 'Own city'	Giedrius Bielskus	Regular, competitive, mass participation	Competitive/ nature	2,000
	Citadele Kaunas marathon 2010	Kauno maratono klubas/ Kaunas Marathon Club	Regimantas Tarasevičius	Regular, competitive, mass participation	International/ Competitive/city	4,000
The Netherlands	Brandloyalty Vestingloop 2006	Artishock	Artishock	Regular, competitive, mass participation	Competitive & recreational/city	5,000
	Marathon Amersfoort 1986	Foundation Marathon Amersfoort	Foundation Marathon Amersfoort, execution committee	Regular, competitive, mass participation	Competitive & recreational/city	5–6,000

and ambitions of event organisers and represent a form of public audit of what has been proclaimed as a result of staging the event and what was actually delivered. A key concept in understanding running events impacts discussed is that of public value. This concept suggests that any impact of running events becomes possible due to the interactions between a valued object (i.e., the running event) and a valuing subject (i.e., the event-specific public). The main concepts discussed in the chapter are further elaborated through the cases of the LifeSouth Race Weekend, Gainesville, Florida, by Kiriaki Kiplianidou and the impact of running events in China by Xiaoyan Xing and Yue Liu.

Finally, Chapter 5 draws some conclusions about the interplay between running events policies, promotion and impacts and provides suggestions for future research.

References

Andrews, H., & Leopold, T. (2013). *Events and the social sciences*. London: Routledge.

Bale, J. (2004). *Running cultures. Racing in time and space*. London: Routledge.

Bowdin, G., McPherson, G., & Flinn, J. (2006). Identifying and analysing existing research undertaken in the events industry: A literature review for People1st Undertaken on behalf of the Association for Events Management Education (AEME).

Capsi, J., & Llopis-Goig, R. (2021). Understanding the expansion of running from a social practice theory perspective. A case study focused on the city of Valencia. *Sport in Society*, 1–21. DOI: 10.1080/17430437.2021.1970139

Casado, K., & Santos-Concejero, A. (2017). "The effect of periodisation and training intensity distribution on middle- and long-distance running performance: A systematic review." *International Journal of Sports Physiology and Performance*, 13(9): 1114–1121.

Cheung, R.T., & Ngai, S.P. (2016). Effects of footwear on running economy in distance runners: A meta-analytical review. *Journal of Science and Medicine in Sport*, 19(3): 260–266.

Collier, D., LaPorte, J., & Seawright, J. (2012). Putting typologies to work: Concept formation, measurement, and analytic rigor. *Political Research Quarterly*, 65(1): 217–232.

Corbally, L., Wilkinson, M., & Fothergill, M.A. (2020). Effects of mindfulness practice on performance and factors related to performance in long distance running: A systematic review. *Journal of Clinical Sport Psychology*, 14(4): 376–398. ISSN 1932-9261

Cronin, M. (2003). Projecting the nation through sport and culture: Ireland, Aonach Tailteann and the Irish Free State, 1924–32. *Journal of Contemporary*, 38(3): 395–411.

The many facets of running 15

Delnoij, M. (2004). *Ze zijn gewoon niet te binden. Hardlopers, atletiekverenigingen en de opkomst van lichte gemeenschappen* [They will always run freely. Runners, track and field clubs and the rise of light communities]. Amsterdam: Amsterdam University; unpublished master thesis in sociology.

Eichberg, H. (1998). *Body cultures: Essays on sport, space and identity.* London: Routledge.

England Athletics. (n.d). *Running segments.* Available at https://www.englandathletics.org/insight/our-research/runner-segments/

Filo, K., & Coghan, A. (2016). Exploring the positive psychology domains of well-being activated through charity sport event experiences. *Event Management, 20*(2): 181–199.

Foucault, Michel. 1979. On Governmentality. *Ideology & Consciousness,* 6: 5–21.

Fredline, L., Raybould, M., Jago, L. & Deery, M. (2004). *Triple bottom line event evaluation: Progress toward a technique to assist in planning and managing events in a sustainable manner.* Paper presented at the Tourism State of the Art II Conference, Glasgow, June 2004.

Garcia-Vallejo, A., Albahari, A., Afio-Sanz, V., & Garrido-Moreno, A. (2020). What's behind a marathon? Process management in running events. *Sustainability, 12*: 6000, 1–18.

Getz, D. (2012). *Event studies. Theory, research and policy for planned events.* London: Routledge.

Gratton, C., Dobson, R., & Shibli, S. (2000). The economic importance of major sports events: A case-study of six events. *Managing Leisure, 5*: 17–28.

Handelman, D. (1998). *Models and mirrors: Towards an anthropology of public events.* New York, NY: Berghahn Books.

Hespanhol Junior, L C., van Mechelen, W., Postuma, E., & Verhagen, E. (2016). Health and economic burden of running-related injuries in runners training for an event: A prospective cohort study. *Scandinavian Journal of Medicine & Science in Sports, 26*(9): 1091–1099. DOI: 10.1111/sms.12541.

Jago, L. K., & Shaw, R.N. (1998). A conceptual and differential framework. *Festival Management and Event Tourism, 5*(1/2): 21–32.

Kakouris, N., Yener, N., & Fong, D. (2021). A systematic review of running-related musculoskeletal injuries in runners. *Journal of Sport and Health Science, 10*(5): 13–22.

Kamphorst, T.J., & Roberts, K. (1989). *Trends in sport: A multinational perspective.* Voorhuizen: Giordana Bruno Culemberg.

Kenneally, M., Casado, A., & Santos-Concejero, J. (2018). The effect of periodization and training intensity distribution on middle-and long-distance running performance: A systematic review. *International Journal of Sports Physiology and Performance, 13*(9): 1114–1121.

Koeningstorfer, J. et al. (2017). The legacy of mega sporting events: A systematic review of empirical studies (1997–2016). European Association for Sport Management (Conference proceedings).

Krieger, J. (2021). *Power and politics in world athletics.* London: Routledge.

Llopis-Goig, R., & Llopis-Goig, D. (2012). A sociocultural typology of recreational runners in Spain Apunts. *Educación Física y Deportes, 108*(2) trimestre (April–June): 9–16.

Mair, J., & Whitford, M. (2013). An exploration of events research: Event topics, themes and emerging trends. *International Journal of Event and Festival Management, 4*(1): 6–30. DOI: 10.1108/17582951311307485.

Malchrowicz-Mośko, E., & Poczta, J. (2018). Running as a form of therapy socio-psychological functions of mass running events for men and women. *International Journal of Environmental Research and Public Health, 15*(10): 2262.

Parent, M. M., & Smith-Swan, S. (2012). *Managing major sports events: Theory and practice.* London: Routledge.

Pereira, H.V., Palmeira, A.L., Encantado, J., Marques, M.M., Santos, I., Carraça, E.V., & Teixeira, P.J. (2021) Systematic review of psychological and behavioral correlates of recreational running. *Frontiers in Psychology, 12*: 624783. DOI: 10.3389/fpsyg.2021.624783.

Plymire, D. C. (2004). Positive addiction: Running and human potential in the 1970s. *Journal of Sport History, 31*(3): 297–315.

Rogers, M., & Ryan, R. (2001). The triple bottom line for sustainable community development. *Local Environment, 6*(3): 279–289. DOI: 10.1080/13549830120073275.

Rohm, A.J., Milne, G.R., & McDonald, M.A. (2006). A mixed-method approach for developing market segmentation typologies in the sports industry. *Sport Marketing Quarterly, 15*(1): 29–39.

Scheerder, J., Breedveld, K., & Borgers, J. (2015). Who is doing a run with the running boom? The growth and governance of one of Europe's most popular sport activities. In: J. Scheerder, K. Breedveld & J. Borgers (Eds.). *Running across Europe. The rise and size of one of the largest sport markets* (pp. 1–27). Basingstoke: Palgrave Macmillan.

Scheu, A., & Preuss, H. (2018). The legacy of the Olympic Games from 1896–2016. A systematic review of academic publications. Working papers Series – Meinzer Papers on Sport Economics & Management, 14.

Seuter, M., Pfeiffer, M., Bauer, G., Zentgraf, K., & Kray, C. (2017). Running with technology: Evaluating the impact of interacting with wearable devices on running movement. *Proceedings of the ACM on Interactive, Mobile, Wearable and Ubiquitous Technologies, 1*(3), Article 101(2) (September 2017): 17. DOI: 10.1145/313096.

Shove, E., Pantzar, M., & Watson, M. (2012). *The dynamics of social practice: Everyday life and how it changes.* London: Sage.

Sleeswijk Visser, T. S., van Middelkoop, M., Fokkema, T., & de Vos, R. J. (2021). The socio-economic impact of running-related injuries: A large prospective cohort study. *Scandinavian Journal of Medicine & Science in Sports, 31*(10): 2002–2009.

Uphill, E. (1965). The Egyptian Sed-Festival Rites Author(s): *Journal of Near Eastern Studies*, Oct., 1965, 24(4), Erich F. Schmidt Memorial Issue. Part Two (Oct., 1965), pp. 365–383.

Van der Worp, M.P., Ten Haaf, D.S., van Cingel, R., de Wijer, A., Nijhuis-van der Sanden, M. W., & Staal, J.B. (2015). Injuries in runners: A systematic review on risk factors and sex differences. *PLoS ONE, 10*(2): e0114937. DOI: 10.1371/journal.pone.0114937

Vos, S., & Scheerder, J. (2009). Loopsport in veelvoud. Naar een typologie van loopsporters [The rich spectrum of running. Towards a typology of runners]. In: J. Scheerder & F. Boen (Eds.). *Vlaanderen loopt! Sociaalwetenschappelijk onderzoek naar de loopsportmarkt* [Running in Flanders. The running market from a social science approach] (SBS Series 1). (pp. 267–287). Ghent: Academia Press.

Ziegel, V., & Grossberger, L. (1978). *The non-runner's book. Advice and reassurance for the millions of Americans who want to know 'Is it all right if I don't run?'*. New York: MacMillan.

2 The running eventscape
Developments, runners' profiles and policies

Jeroen Scheerder and Kobe Helsen

Introduction

Over the past five decades, running for recreational purposes has become one of the most popular leisure-time physical activities globally (Scheerder & Breedveld, 2013; Scheerder, Breedveld & Borgers, 2015a). The fact that active involvement in mass participation running has tremendously exploded in popularity can be seen as an indication that forms of physical endurance in a sportive way nowadays are socially praised and well-rewarded by society (Salazar & Scheerder, 2023). Yet, running was already glorified for its characteristics of escape, freedom and pilgrimage long before the so-called running boom started in the second half of the 20th century. Running novelists, such as the English *Angry Young Men* literary movement member Alan Sillitoe (1959), and, later on, also the famous Dutch ultrarunner and historian Jan Knippenberg (1987) and the currently still active Japanese bestselling writer and marathon runner Haruki Murakami (2008), wittily and poignantly applauded the physical hardship and mental loneliness that come with long-distance running. From the 1970s and 1980s onwards, running was perceived as a health-producing lifestyle endeavour, improving one's physical and mental well-being (Bridel et al., 2016).

Ever since, running as a leisurely activity seems to prosper in countries with a neoliberal welfare regime, which could lead to the interpretation that recreational running thrives well in a cultural and political environment where self-actualisation, self-empowerment and self-discipline are regarded as key values (Bridel et al., 2016; Egan-Wyer, 2019; 2023; Llopis-Goig, 2014). At present, however, running needs to be considered as much more than a merely health-enhancing sporting activity based on the value of its cardiovascular capacities (Carter, 2018). As a paramount feature in many people's daily life, running has become a multifaceted, societal phenomenon that encompasses

DOI: 10.4324/9781003301691-2

different and divergent angles. More precisely, leisurely running and event running in particular are valued for their social, cultural and health-related qualities, as well as for economic gain and political assets. Because of these benefits, running events of various kinds pullulate at present, both in number and in diversity, culminating in and contributing to the eventscape[1] as can be witnessed nowadays. In addition, running in an organised and collective manner is enabled by a variety of actors where each aims at profits of a different kind, including civil society organisations, public authorities, commercial providers and self-organised, light communities. That is why event running is also attractive to huge and distinct crowds of both participants and spectators, and thus has unfurled itself into a flourishing business on an international scale (Breedveld & Scheerder, 2017; Funk et al., 2016, pp. 30–31).

This chapter will first map out the running industry by outlining the rise of the running market, as well as some key developments. For this, we will make use of long-term international data, if available, supplemented with recent survey material, among which are the outcomes and insights from the European *Run for Health* research project[2] (Alexandris et al., 2021; Helsen & Scheerder, 2020; Helsen et al., 2020; for more details see also Chapter 1 and later in this chapter). As the focus of the present book is on running events, we will mainly rely on data related to running as an organised leisure-time physical activity. Building on these analyses, hereafter, the focus will be on the social profile of recreational runners, inasmuch sociodemographic characteristics as sex, age and social status are concerned. Here, again, existing data from mainly cross-temporal and cross-national investigations will be used, and, if possible, further supplemented. As such, a contemporary picture of the running industry, its providers as well as its consumers, will be presented. Finally, the chapter will interrogate the position and role of different actors in the running market. More precisely, this section of the chapter will deal with the policy and governance issues from a multi-actors' approach. Here, emphasis is put in particular on the concept of public value, as running events are said to be in a good position to significantly add value to the public sphere by reaching out beyond mere market economic logics (see also Chapter 4). At the end of the chapter, two specific case studies, related to three of the most popular running events in Belgium, are included dealing with trends and runners' profiles at the one hand, and event policies and marketing on the other. Based on the insights provided in the present chapter, these case studies will offer the reader a specific understanding into these events.

Developments in the running industry

Three waves of running

So far, three post-WWII waves of running can be distinguished in the development of recreational distance running (Hover, 2013; Scheerder, 2017; Scheerder et al., 2015b). Prior to the three running waves, however, running was a sporting activity almost exclusively practised by competitive athletes in private clubs, or at schools or universities through extracurricular programmes (Bale, 2004). For the greater part of the 20th century, running for recreational purposes in public, apart from club and school settings, was a rather unusual physical activity. Nevertheless, from the late 1960s, leisurely running would increasingly find its way out of athletic clubs and educational institutions, and would gain an independent status, separate from the track and field court, and pursued in the public sphere. This running movement was initiated by young urban professionals, predominantly males, and resulted in the first, so-called running boom. The first running wave originated in the US, and later came over to Europe. It would last from the late 1960s through the beginning of the 1980s (Scheerder et al., 2015b; Van Bottenburg, Scheerder & Hover, 2010). At the time, running as a sporting activity had undergone a transformation along with the processes of *de-traditionalisation* (Heelas, 1996) and *de-sportification* (Crum, 1993). Actually, these two processes imply that leisurely running turned from a competitive sporting activity in a club-organised setting mainly practised by a relatively small number of *athletes*, into a recreational pastime that would attract large numbers of *joggers* and *runners* practising running on their own or in the so-called light communities (Scheerder et al., 2015b; Van Bottenburg, 2006; see also Smith, 1998). In relation to this, Atkinson (2010) refers to the concept of 'post-sport athletics', meaning that a de-centring of traditional sporting forms, such as track and field, had taken place by means of the introduction of non-mainstream physical cultural practices, like road running, that do not necessarily replicate hyper-competitive, rule-bound and hierarchical features as in modern sports. Making running a less competitive physical activity implied that more and more people would enjoy running as a leisure-time pursuit without the need to fulfil strict playing rules and formal standards. The cultural revolution of the 1960s and 1970s, characterised, among other things, by a process of *informalisation* of everyday behaviour and habits (Wouters, 2007), went hand in hand with the fitness revolution and the recreational revolution in sport, in particular with regard to road running (Sánchez García,

2019; Scheerder, 2007; Stokvis, 2005; Vanreusel, 1984). As such, leisurely running contributed to the fact that more and more people felt at ease when being physically active in public. Although blown over from the US as a relatively new form of leisure-time physical activity, the first wave of running was largely underpinned by the Sport for All policies that had a major breakthrough in Europe at the late 1960s and during the 1970s (Breedveld & Scheerder, 2017). Actually, leisure-time running seemed to perfectly match with the aims of the Sport for All movement since running was perceived as a type of sportive activity that is easy to organise and that requires hardly any technical skills nor sophisticated facilities. Moreover, running also met the objectives stated by public welfare policies in terms of both health promotion and social integration. As a consequence, in many European countries, public campaigns were launched to stimulate running among their residents. As such, public authorities played a key role in stimulating the growth of recreational running. Germany, Finland and Denmark, for instance, held their first mass running events in, respectively, 1963, 1966 and 1969 (Breedveld et al., 2015). Furthermore, specific campaigns to promote running were initiated in The Netherlands in 1968 ('Trim Actie'), in Germany in 1970 ('Trimm Dich') and in Hungary in 1972 ('Run for your Health') (Breedveld et al., 2015). Thus, the first boom of recreational runners starting at the end of the 1960s came when governments commenced to focusing on mass sport as part of their newly established welfare and health policies (see Scheerder et al., 2011; Van Bottenburg et al., 2005; Vanreusel & Taks, 1998). Soon after, mass running organised across the streets became a familiar sight in European cities, with annual marathon events initiated in Athens (1972), Berlin (1974), Amsterdam (1975), Paris (1976), Madrid (1978), Stockholm (1979), Warsaw (1979), Barcelona (1980), Dublin (1980), Frankfurt (1981), Helsinki (1981), London (1981), Rotterdam (1981), Rome (1982), Budapest (1984), Reykjavik (1984), Vienna (1984), Lisbon (1986), etc. (adapted chronological list of European city marathons based on Scheerder et al., 2015b).

On its turn, the second running wave took a start at the end of the 20th century. By then, running, as a mass leisure-time physical activity, had successfully spread from the US to Europe, and it was gaining ground in other continents as well, especially in Asia (Scheerder et al., 2015b; see also below). During the second wave of running, at the start of the 21st century, new groups of participants entered the running market. More specifically, running had undergone a social and demographic transition since significantly more women and older people started running in their spare time (Scheerder & Boen, 2009;

Van Bottenburg et al., 2010; Van Dyck et al., 2017). This evolution can be seen in part as a democratisation of leisurely running, at least in terms of sex and age. However, as we will show later, according to socio-cultural and socio-economic background, it is noteworthy that social disparities persist, as running still appears to be a middle-class sporting activity (Scheerder et al., 2015a; Scheerder & Thibaut, 2021b). As a result of this (partial) democratisation process, a huge running industry had emerged, ranging from technologically advanced running shoes, equipment and running accessories, to increasingly marketed running events attracting growing numbers of participants, both competitive and recreational (Breedveld & Scheerder, 2017, see also Thibaut et al., 2021b). From this, also a tourist industry with a focus on running events was born, decoying participants from different corners around the world (McGehee et al., 2003; Rauter & Topic, 2014). Actually, running, as a leisure-time physical activity, has gone through a process of commodification, which has led to the commercialisation of big and new running events that we see nowadays. Running for recreational purposes had become a commodity because runners were willing not only to spend time on it but also to pay for actively participating in it. Wearing and Wearing (1992) stated that running from a simple physical activity had been transformed into a multi-million dollars industry with many sectors. In fact, these authors anticipated what would become a common practice in the world of recreational running during the upcoming decades:

> The joy of jogging will be enhanced, the advertising suggests, by choosing the best from an array of coloured, cushioned, even computerized shoes, which tell you how far you have run, in what time, at what pace and how many calories you have consumed.
> (Wearing & Wearing, 1992, p. 3)

While running, and running events in particular, in the 1970s and 1980s was mainly organised by cities and athletic clubs, commercial agents, at the end of the 20th century, had partly taken over and had developed their own running events, and even running clubs and communities (Breedveld & Scheerder, 2017). No longer, (local) governments nor athletic clubs held a monopoly on organising running events, indicating a partly shift from recreational running as a commonly and publicly owned good to a privately controlled product. This is not to say, however, that public and non-profit organisations would not play a significant role anymore in promoting and supporting running as a leisure-time physical activity. On the contrary, (local) governments continue to invest in running and running events, for instance, by providing public running facilities such as running circuits and tracks (Breedveld & Scheerder, 2017). The commercialisation and commodification of recreational running can be illustrated by means of the development of city runs, such as city marathons have gone through. More precisely, it is clear that during the second wave of running, cities and municipalities have welcomed a more marketing-driven approach, i.e. in terms of place marketing, in order to better position themselves as key players in the promotion of health and physical activity. Moreover, the rise of recreational running as a commodity, along with the processes of individualisation and globalisation, has introduced new forms of public policies, implying that more attention has been paid to issues such as social equality, safety, environmental protection and personal health. This resulted in a running industry open not only to larger groups of participants, but also to new segments of participants, in particular women and middle-aged people. As a consequence, these developments have also fostered the consumption of running, including running equipment and apparel, and thus also have created economic growth (for an illustration on this regarding the evolution of the running industry in China, see the second case study in Chapter 4). Speaking in terms of a running business, city marathons like the London Marathon and the New York City Marathon attract tens of thousands of spectators who line the city streets to cheer on the masses of participants, and are also watched by millions of viewers and followers worldwide.

While some stagnation, in terms of participatory numbers, could be noticed between the first and second running waves (Scheerder et al., 2015b, see also further), so far, no such form of a longer-lasting flattening, let alone a sharp or significant decline in the number of runners or running events, has occurred after the second wave of running. One could therefore argue that the second running wave is still on its way. However, based on cultural, economic and social changes that became visible from the second decade of the 21st century, some authors have already signalled the emergence during that decade of a third wave of running (Breedveld & Scheerder, 2017; Hover, 2013; Hover et al., 2015; Janssen, 2022; Patty, 2016; Scheerder et al., 2015b). While the first and second waves of running mainly focused on road running, the third wave can be characterised as adding an extra dimension to the running sportscape, and the eventscape in particular, based on the introduction of three key developments. First, the rapid growth of urban, nature and theme running events, such as urban trails, obstacle races, mud runs, colour runs and the like, is remarkable (Patty, 2016; Weedon, 2016). This type of non-traditional running events is almost similar to music festivals, including a stage, sounds and spot lights. Parallel to this trend of what could be determined as the 'festivalisation' of running, also the rise of extreme running races and related feats is obvious. Here, one could think of ultrarunning, among which are desert runs, fell and mountain runs, trail runs and ultramarathons (Atkinson, 2016; Kurtoglu-Hooton, 2021; Lanclus, 2023; McKay et al., 2019; Ronto, 2021). Thus, it seems that running events partly have followed a trend towards a process of 'extremisation'. Of course, extreme running endeavours have already a longstanding tradition, but the remarkable thing here is that they have become more popular, in such a way that nowadays this kind of running events is attended by larger and more diverse groups of participants than was the case before. A third and most recent development within the third running wave can be described as the process of 'self-quantification', or the birth of the 'quantified running self' as we would call it (see also Helsen et al., 2022; Janssen et al., 2017; 2020). By means of self-monitoring applications, such as FitoTrack, Runalyze, RunKeeper or Strava, individual running performances are registered, analysed and shared on social media. Running participants as well as running providers eagerly welcome technologically mediated surveillance encouraging digital self-tracking and bodily self-discipline (Couture, 2021). As a consequence, running event organisers more and more tend to provide flat, straight and fast running courses, so that participants are able to run and optimise their personal best time.

Having these three developments of festivalisation, extremisation and self-quantification in mind, it may be of no surprise that along with the third running wave go the processes of commercialisation, professionalisation, digitalisation and virtualisation. Although different in kind, the processes of commercialisation and professionalisation go hand in hand. At present, running has been transformed into a highly marketed product as companies tend to take over much of the most popular running events (Breedveld & Scheerder, 2017), while at the same time have drawn these events closer to what Pine and Gilmore (1999) have referred to as the experience economy. Theatre-like elements are introduced in running events, procreating authentic bodily experiences. As such, lived experiences are consumed by masses of running participants. Moreover, fuelled by the COVID-19 pandemic, the processes of digitalisation and virtualisation have had an extra impact, both on running in general and on running events in particular (Helsen et al., 2021). In Table 2.1, a schematic overview of the three waves concerning the development of post-WWII leisure-time running and their characteristics are presented.

Table 2.1 Different waves in the development of post-WWII recreational running

Wave	Period	Generation	Trend/Revolution	Setting/Locus	Form	Actor	Aim/Adage	Social group	Icon/Emblem
0	<1970s	Builders	standardisation *sportification*	stadium	track & field	athlete	competition/ training	Club	Chronometer
1	1970s–1980s	Boomers/ Yuppies	de-traditionalisation *cultural revolution*	road	road run	runner	completion/ recreation	Individual	Sweatband
2	1990s–2000s	Busters	democratisation *social revolution*	city	city run	jogger	healthiness/ sociability	Light community	Chip
3	2010s–present	Bridgers/ Millennials/ Yolos	scene-isation *digital revolution*	stage	festival/ adventure/ Race	party-goer/ hero/ racer	sensation/ performance	Digital tribe	Wearable

Running waves in numbers

By making use of available time-trend data, the different waves of running can be empirically illustrated. However, databases that contain long-lasting statistics on (event) running allowing for drawing analyses from both an international and cross-temporal perspective hardly exist (Scheerder et al., 2015b, p. 8). Generally, available numbers are country-specific, incomplete or even inaccurate, and therefore cannot be used for comparative analyses. Nonetheless, statistical data on marathoning do appear to be largely available. Time-trend data on marathoning are relatively easy to access as this type of running focuses on one particular and iconic type of running event. Until 2017, the *Association of Road Racing Statisticians* (ARRS) provided a wealth of running data, mainly on marathon races and finishers (Milroy et al., 2018). As a consequence, based on worldwide ARRS data for both the number of marathon events and the number of marathon finishers, it is possible to identify waves 1 and 2 (see Figure 2.1). As indicated before, running wave 1 started in the late 1960s and lasted until the beginning of the 1980s. In this period, as shown in Figure 2.1, the number of marathon events multiplied by almost five and the number of marathon finishers multiplied by even more than a hundred. The second wave of mass participation running is said to be initiated at the end

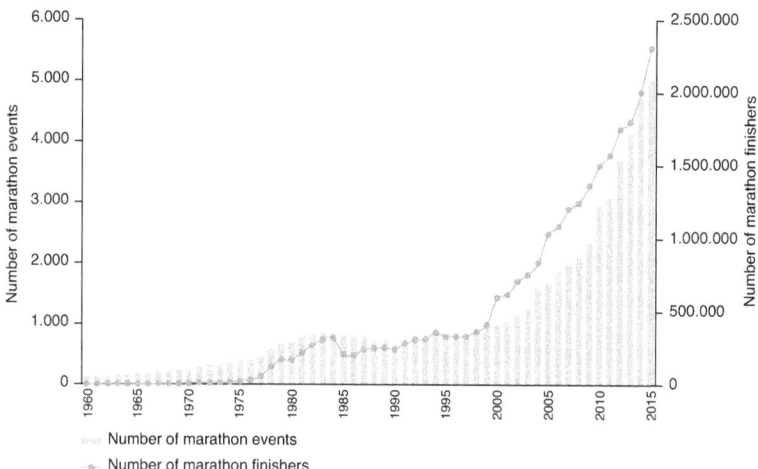

Figure 2.1 Number of marathon events and finishers, worldwide data (1960–2015).

Source: Authors' own calculations based on www.arrs.run and Scheerder et al. (2015b).

of the 20th century. As can be deferred from Figure 2.1, the number of marathon events has almost tripled between 1999 and 2009. In this time interval, the number of marathon finishers has even multiplied by more than three. From Figure 2.1, we also learn that, for most of the 1980s and 1990s, both the number of marathon events and the number of marathon finishers almost stagnated. This demarcates the phase of transition between the first and second waves of running. During this transition, the daily average of marathons was equal to two, while in the second wave of running, the number of marathons organised on average each day would more than double, from nearly three in 1999 to more than six in 2009[3] (Scheerder et al., 2015b). It is, however, noteworthy that during the transition phase, the number of participants in the world's 20 largest marathons continued to rise (see Figure 2.2), while at the same time the total number of finishers thus remained almost the same (supra). One can therefore state that, between the first and second running waves, the globally most popular city marathons have strengthened their total share in terms of participatory numbers.

As previously indicated, the third running wave seems to commence from the second decade of the 21st century onwards. It builds on the second wave, implying that both the number of events and the number

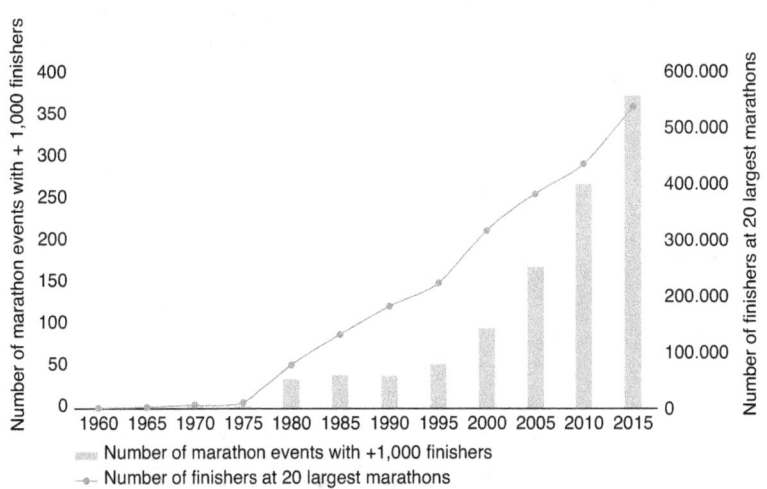

Figure 2.2 Number of marathon events with more than 1,000 finishers and number of finishers at 20 largest marathons, worldwide data (1960–2015).

Source: Authors' own calculations based on www.arrs.run and Scheerder et al. (2015b).

of participants are still increasing (Capsi & Llopis-Goig, 2021; Hover, 2013; Scheerder et al., 2015a). But, parallel to this ongoing accretion, the character of running events has changed remarkably due to the processes of product diversification, commercialisation, digitalisation and the like (supra). As we mentioned, data presented in Figures 2.1 and 2.2 relate to marathoning. Worldwide data on recreational running in general, thus including running distances other than marathons, are rather sparse and/or imprecise, particularly from a time-trend perspective. This makes it hard to delineate the third wave of running. Nevertheless, running data collected by World Athletics (Andersen, 2021; Andersen & Nikolova, s.a.) allow us to have a glance on how mass participation in event running has evolved over the last two decades. More precisely, the statistical report by Andersen and Nikolova (s.a.) states that participation in running races peaked in 2016 with a total of 9.1 million finishers, underlining the continued popularity of event running worldwide. However, event participation appears to be in a decline since 2016, as the number of running participants dropped to 7.9 million in 2018.[4] Thus, it seems that for the first time a peak in running participants has been reached as mass participation running is likely to decline after 2016. A trend report by Running USA seems to confirm this tendency as the number of people registering for the US road races declined with almost 5% between 2016 and 2019 (Running USA, 2020; numbers not presented). As can be noted from Figure 2.3, however, the number of arrivals at the top 100 road races in the US does not appear to dwindle over the past two decades, despite a

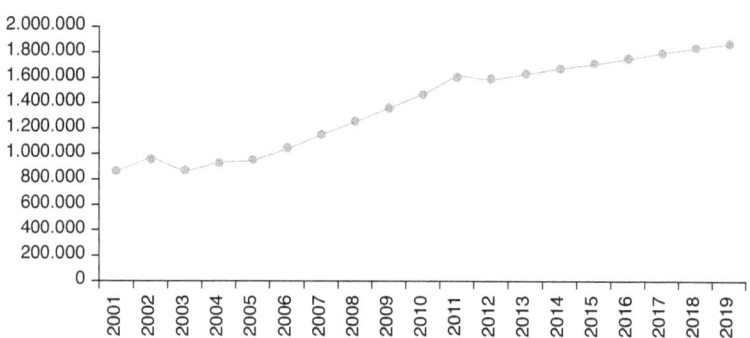

Figure 2.3 Number of finishers at the 100 largest road races in the US (2001–2019).

Source: Authors' own calculations based on www.runsignup.blog, www.runningusa. org and Scheerder et al. (2015b).

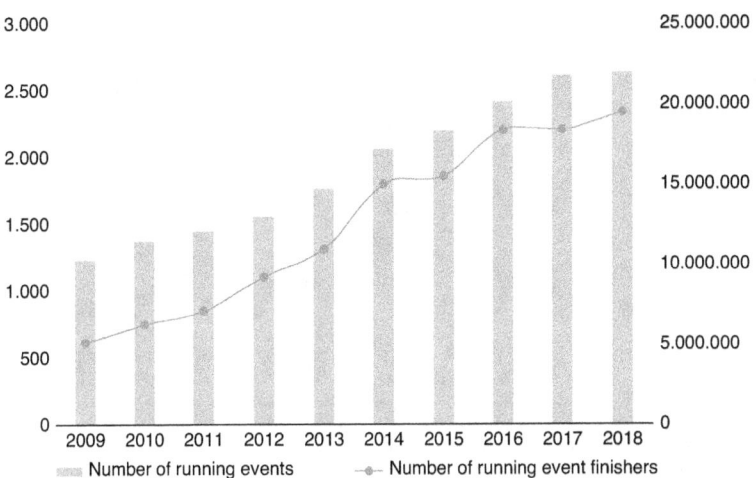

Figure 2.4 Number of running events and finishers in Japan (2009–2018).
Source: Authors' own calculations with support of Ding Yi Wu (Waseda University, Japan).

relative slowdown since 2011. In Japan also, as shown in Figure 2.4, no significant retrogression in the number of running events or the number of finishers can be registered over the past decade. The same goes for Flanders, Belgium, where no decline can be noted for the last decade in terms of the number of running events, the number of running event finishers, as well as the general number of runners (Figure 2.5). It is, of course, too early to draw firm conclusions as the time interval of the possible decline, so far, only covers a few years. Moreover, other sources have signalled a likely revival of recreational running during and/or due to the COVID-19 pandemic (Helsen et al., 2021; Rizzo, 2021; Strava, 2020; Thibaut et al., 2021a). Again, these data only reflect a snapshot and need a further and deeper investigation to confirm a possible trend.

As Andersen and Nikolova (s.a.) suggest, the decline in running participation is mainly due to a diminution in Europe and the US. In Asia, however, a rapid growth continues. This is also apparent from Table 2.2 which shows the marathon market shares at a continental level. In 2015, Asia held the highest share of marathon arrivals, equalling 38% (up from just a share of 2% in 2000 and less than 1% in 1980). These percentages, however, can be seen as an underrepresentation, as Asia's proportion of the world population equals 60%. This can also

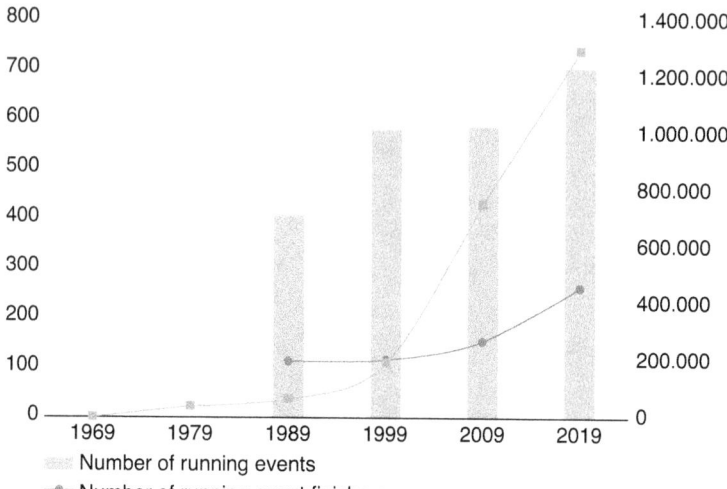

Figure 2.5 Number of running events, finishers and runners in Flanders, Belgium (1969–2019).
Source: Authors' own calculations based on Borgers et al. (2015), Helsen and Scheerder (2022) and Scheerder and Thibaut (2021c).

Table 2.2 Continental marathon market shares in 1980, 2000 and 2015, in percentages

	Share of marathon arrivals			Share of marathon events			Share world population	Share world population	Share world population
	1980	2000	2015	1980	2000	2015	1980	2000	2015
Europe	14.5	41.5	31.4	30.9	45.6	53.9	15.6	11.8	10.1
North America	82.3	54.0	25.5	51.8	32.7	25.7	5.7	5.1	4.8
Asia	0.4	2.3	38.4	4.6	10.4	14.2	59.4	60.9	60.1
rest	2.8	2.3	4.7	12.8	11.2	6.3	19.3	22.2	25.0

Source: Authors' own calculations based on www.arrs.net, https://population.un.org/wpp/Download/Standard/Population/ and Scheerder et al. (2015b).

be interpreted as an indication for travel tourism related to running events, as the share of marathon events held in Asia only covers 14%. Thus, with less than one-fifth of the marathon events, Asian marathons reach out to more than a third of the marathon runners. The highest shares of marathon events in the first, second and third waves of running, however, still belong to the US (52% in 1980) and Europe (46% in 2000 and 54% in 2015). Travelling to running events has never been more popular as the proportion of people participating in a running race abroad has significantly increased, as also evidenced in the first case study of the present chapter. This is especially the case for marathoning, as the global share of foreign registrants for marathon events has augmented from 0.2% in 1994 to 3.5% in 2018 (Andersen, 2021). Here, one could think of the *World Marathon Majors*, a series of six world-class city marathons, including the Tokyo Marathon, the Boston Marathon, the London Marathon, the Berlin Marathon, the Chicago Marathon and the New York City Marathon, for which in total over 100,000 entrants register each year. Contrary to the apparently levelling off in the participation in 5Ks, 10Ks and (half) marathons (supra), participation in ultrarunning has undergone a strong increase. According to Ronto (2021), participation in ultrarunning has exploded from 34,401 yearly participations in 1996 to 611,098 in 2018. Especially since 2008, the growth rate of ultrarunning participation has tremendously increased, and has even surpassed that of 5Ks and marathons.

Runners' profiles

Demographics

Rather than focusing too much on the recent but still somewhat limited data, it is of more relevance to look at the underlying developments to discern a current new wave of running. From the World Athletics data (Andersen, 2021; Andersen & Nikolova, s.a.), it is clear that event runners have never been older, as their average age changed from 35.2 years in 1986 to 39.3 years in 2018. Consequently, the average speed at running events has lowered (see also the first case study related to the present chapter). Also, for the first time in the global history of running, slightly more female than male runners participate in running events (50.2% vs. 49.8%). It is however remarkable that a clear gender difference exists according to the running distance. Based on the European *Run for Health* research project (Alexandris et al., 2021; Helsen & Scheerder, 2020), in which running data were collected for five European countries, including Flanders (Belgium), Greece, Italy, Lithuania and The Netherlands, it is apparent that in 2019 women are more likely to dominate in short distances ($x < 5$ km), while men prevail in medium (5 km $> x < 16.2$ km) and long ($x > 16.2$ km) distances. This is in line with the findings from the global World Athletics report

(Andersen, 2021; Andersen & Nikolova, s.a.). Thus, from a heavily male-dominated sporting activity, mass participation running has evolved into a more female-friendly physical activity. This development can be related to the success of specific running events and programmes, such as ladies runs and start to run initiatives, that have been launched by both profit and non-profit providers. The fact that the male-female ratio is gradually shifting in favour of women is also noticeable when looking at the data on marathoning, which can be considered a fairly elite form of running. Figure 2.6 shows that, prior to the second wave of running, i.e. before the end of the 20th century, it was not uncommon to see more than ten male marathoners for every female marathoner. After 2010, in almost all countries included in Figure 2.6, the male vs. female ratio has lowered to less than 10:1, which is an indication that the share of female marathon finishers is obviously on the rise.

Motives for running

Parallel to the demographic transitions outlined in the previous section, also a shift occurred regarding the motives for running.

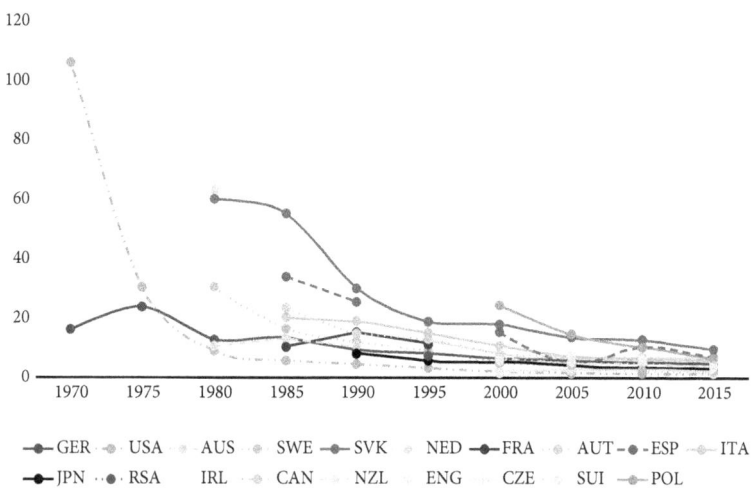

Figure 2.6 Evolution of male/female ratios for marathon participation in different countries (1970–2015).[5]

Source: Authors' own calculations based on www.arrs.run, Helsen and Scheerder (2020) and Scheerder et al. (2015b).

According to Andersen and Nikolova (s.a.), new segments of runners prefer a nice running experience to a merely individual physical achievement, the latter being for a long time the predominant motivation for participating in running events. Thus, along with competition-driven athletes and runners, now also experience-oriented joggers and racers have entered the world of running. From the findings of the *Run for Health* project, we also learn that, currently, 'competition' is the least important motive for runners to participate in a running event, whereas drivers such as excitement and socialising significantly rank higher (Alexandris et al., 2021; Helsen & Scheerder, 2020). Moreover, as a result of the developments described, event organisers have broadened or even adapted their offerings by introducing new running formulas, such as urban, nature and theme running events (supra). The *Run for Health* project has shown that in 2019 more than two-thirds (65%) of the event runners prefer urban running events (city runs, urban trails, local joggings, etc.), followed by nature running events, like obstacle runs, beach runs, trail runs (25%), and theme running events such as ladies runs, colour runs and Santa runs (17%) (Helsen & Scheerder, 2020). The results from the *Run for Health* project also indicate that the vast majority of the event runners (58%) are not practising their sport based on a membership of a sports club, while only 23% of the event runners does mention to be a member of an athletic club. Moreover, again according to the findings of the *Run for Health* study, almost one-fifth (17%) of the running eventers participates in an informal running group. In their respective cross-national comparative studies, Breedveld et al. (2015) and Van Bottenburg et al. (2010) have already shown that recreational runners largely practise their sport on their own, in the companionship of their friends and family, and/or in nonformal networks, often referred to as light running communities. This means that the market share of athletic clubs and federations is diminishing, as they represent a declining proportion of the total number of people taking part in recreational running. Or in other words, less traditional environments and less formal settings in which people practise running, especially running events in all their variety, have grown in popularity, hence the continuation and even intensification of the already described processes of de-traditionalisation and informalisation during the third wave of running (supra). This can also be interpreted as an organisational shift in the policies of profit and non-profit providers, as contemporary forms of running have increased their share at the expense of traditional running races and championships.

Social status

Apart from sex and age, and also the level of running participation, the motive(s) for participating in running and the running setting in which one is participating (supra), the social position of the running participants deserves attention as well. To our knowledge, however, it seems that hardly any time-trend statistics from an international perspective are available when it comes to make cross-national and cross-temporal comparisons with regard to the social status of running participants. As yet, to obtain reliable empirical data on the socio-cultural and the socio-economic status of running as a leisure-time physical activity, we are dependent on country-specific data. One such research instrument that enables us to analyse to what extent recreational running has spread across different social layers is the so-called social status pyramid of sport, in which specific sports practices are related to the participants' socio-professional status (Renson, 1976; Scheerder et al., 2002). The sports pyramid is based on sports participation survey data collected among households in Flanders, Belgium. So far, the social status pyramid has been composed based on six time-intervals, ever since 1969, and therefore allows for a multi-decade time-trend analysis (Scheerder & Thibaut, 2021b). From Figure 2.7, it can be observed that participating in recreational running is characteristic for middle-class people. As one can see, two running-related figures can be distinguished in the pyramid, including one figure in black and the other in grey. The difference between the two relates to running in a club-organised setting on the one hand (figure in black), and to running outside a club on the other (figure in grey). Based on their social positions, we can state that club-organised running for recreational purposes, (i.e. recreational running by means of a membership of a track and field club) appears to be a less democratised activity, since club-organised running ranks higher on the social status pyramid compared to recreational running in general. Moreover, still based on the survey data collected in Flanders (Belgium), Scheerder and Thibaut (2021b) have shown that, across the past decades, running as a leisure-time physical activity hardly underwent a process of social mobility, neither downwardly nor upwardly. So, despite its growing popularity over the past half-century, recreational running did not significantly change its social appeal as it continues to be a physical pastime that is mainly practised by middle-class people. Consequently, no trickle-down or trickle-up effect can be detected. Rather, a trickling-across diffusion process has taken place, as partaking in recreational running has mainly become more popular among middle-class groups,

The running eventscape 35

Figure 2.7 Social status pyramid of sports participation in Flanders, Belgium, according to socio-professional status.
Source: Scheerder and Thibaut (2021a).

but hardly among upper and lower social layers. Further research, however, is needed to confirm whether these empirical insights also count for other countries. Based on the European *Run for Health* data, however, it is already clear that almost eight out of ten event runners have a higher educational background (Helsen & Scheerder, 2020).[6] Thus, in general, no democratisation pattern can be observed when it comes to the participation in recreational running, be it in an organised or non-organised setting.

The fact that recreational running seems to appeal more to people with a rather higher social status is somewhat curious, given that the practice of it does not necessarily require high spending, expensive gear or the use of purpose-built facilities. From a Bourdieusian (1978; 1984) lens, participation in recreational running can be seen as a social class-related expression of maintaining an active lifestyle. Middle-aged, higher-educated people are most likely to pursuing both a busy and healthy lifestyle as they have a high sense and need for individual control over their time budget and personal health (Breedveld et al., 2015). Providers such as commercial agents and local municipalities are well aware of these benefits, and therefore put extra emphasis in their policies to stimulate and organise health-enhancing physical activities like small-scale and/or easily accessible running initiatives. People who highly engage in regular physical activity and fast-growing individual sports practices such as recreational running, but also fitness and swimming, belong to the so-called 'active class' (Scheerder et al., 2015b). Florida (2012) has coined this group of consumers with the term 'creative class'. Members of this social class prefer leisure activities in which they can deploy self-discipline and self-investment. Moreover, they have a strong interest in physical and mental health, physical appearance, bodily experiences and the companionship of other upper-status persons. Recreational running fits well into this picture since it offers opportunities to remain healthy in a time-effective way, while having the feeling to be part of a larger running community. As such, running can be considered a social status symbol as it is associated with a healthy and well-managed way of life.

Policy actors in the running market

Role of running providers

Currently, mass running has become a multi-billion business (Breedveld et al., 2015). In fact, a gigantic running industry exists in which multiple actors with different profit orientations play a significant role. Generally, recreational running is made possible through a range of providers, including commercial sports companies, national and local authorities, and athletic clubs and federations. Each of these providers belongs to a specific sector, including the commercial sector, the public sector and the voluntary or third sector, respectively, and subscribes to different philosophies. Based on the so-called multi-profit model, a schematic overview of these sectors in relation to the business of running is given in Figure 2.8. Traditionally, (sports) organisations are classified on the

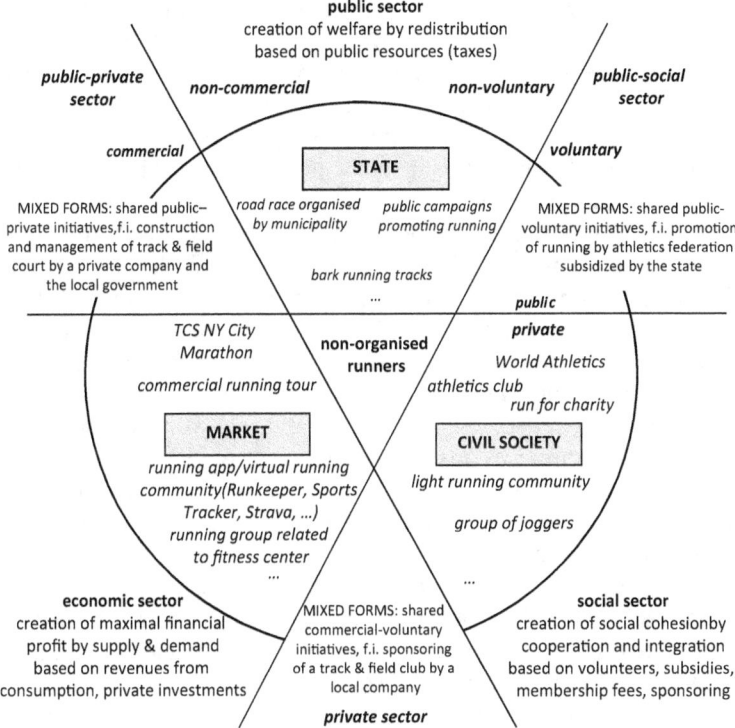

Figure 2.8 Multi-sector model for the organisation and provision of recreational running.
Source: Authors' adaptation based on Borgers et al. (2015, p. 30) and Scheerder (2020, p. 158).

basis of different criteria, among which are their profit orientation, the source of funding and the prime beneficiary. Athletic clubs and federations belong to the third sector and, as such, are largely dependent on volunteers and governmental subsidies for providing their services. The findings from the *Run for Health* research project show that, similar to the situation over a decade ago (see Van Bottenburg et al., 2010), European athletic federations and their clubs, by means of their policies and programmes, still fail to adequately respond to the needs of recreational runners and apparently face difficulties in reaching out to new and potential segments of runners (Alexandris et al., 2021; Helsen et al., 2020). When it comes to long-distance running, the main focus of most of the European federations continues to be on competitive forms of running, such as road race championships and cross-country competitions.

Although there are examples of running initiatives aiming for less active people, such as start to run programmes, athletic clubs and federations still struggle to effectively attract non-competitive runners or to keep them on board. This is somewhat noteworthy, considering that, in particular from a health-enhancing perspective, high benefits can be gained from the recreational segment of runners. Although clubs and federations seem to have missed the running boat (Van Bottenburg et al., 2010), it would be incorrect not to recognise the role that clubs and federations have played, or even still play, in the organisation and management of running, and running events in particular. Athletic clubs have originated many of today's running events. However, the largest running events are usually too big for clubs to manage and have therefore been gradually taken over and run by commercial companies (Breedveld & Scheerder, 2017). Also, new and innovative products, especially theme running events such as colour runs and ladies runs, are mainly in the hands of commercial providers. This shows that the commercialisation of the running industry is still ongoing and that lucrative parts of the running market are usurped by corporate players as a commodity to make further financial profits. For instance, in Belgium and The Netherlands, previously popular running events provided by athletic clubs run on a voluntary basis are being gradually taken over by commercial agents during the past two decades. This is hardly a surprise as, parallel to the popularity of recreational running, participants appear to have a relatively high willingness to pay for running events, as well as for related services and goods such as side events and a photo or even film coverage (Grant & Teahan, 2019; Söderberg, 2014; Wicker & Hallmann, 2013).

Despite the ongoing commodification and commercialisation of the running industry, yet, a substantial amount of running events is still in the hands of local athletic clubs. For example, in Flanders (Belgium), only a minority of all running events (6%) are commercially exploited. However, this minority mainly concerns major running events, that, moreover, account for almost half of all of the arrivals (45%) at running events in Flanders, which implies a multiplication by more than ten between 2004 and 2019 (authors own calculations; see also Borgers et al., 2015, p. 38). Nevertheless, the societal role that athletic clubs play in terms of providing (smaller) running events cannot be underestimated. Athletic clubs, as other sports clubs, heavily rely on the social capital generated through their volunteers. Thanks to the democratic fabric of sports clubs and their respective umbrella organisations, club members have the opportunity to actively participate in the decision-making process regarding their favourite sport, and thus to contribute to public welfare (Elmose-Østerlund et al., 2020, see also Hoekman et al., 2015). In addition, for many runners the first running experiences in their live began at the local athletic club or at school through extracurricular running competitions. Thus, for many youngsters to become familiar with running, athletic clubs play a vital role, particularly from a perspective of socialisation and social integration. So, it is needless to stress that athletic clubs, being a specific form of civil society association, have the potential to fulfil a significant social role in the running industry in particular, and in society in general. This is not to mention, however, that athletic clubs and federations could be even much more involved in the industry of running events, in particular with regard to communities of recreational runners (Breedveld et al., 2015; Scheerder et al., 2015b; Van Bottenburg et al., 2010).

Role of the public sector

Along with the commercial and voluntary running providers, another important stakeholder in the running industry concerns the public sector. In the context of this chapter, we mean national and local governments. Governments and their agencies do not only grant subsidies to (non-)profit organisations in order to receive services that they cannot deliver, or do not have to deliver according to the principle of subsidiarity. Public authorities have a mandate to promote a healthy lifestyle among their residents, and have been making smart use of the benefits that a popular, health-enhancing physical activity such as recreational running offers. That is why governments are, among others, (partly) involved in the management of running events and of running facilities. As regards the latter, one may think of specific running infrastructures, such as athletic tracks, but also the so-called 'bark running tracks' (see f.i. Borgers et al., 2016) and other forms of light running facilities in public parks and forests of which runners can make use freely and whenever they want. Of course, cities and municipalities are also involved in the management of running events from a (destination) marketing perspective. Well-known examples here are the major international city marathons like those of New York City, London or Tokyo, but also smaller running events at national and local levels where mostly commercial companies closely cooperate with governments. However, when providing running services to the public, it is of utmost importance not only to gain economic profits, but ultimately to create public value.

Public value and the need for collaboration

Public authorities have an undeniable responsibility for creating public value, a concept that will also be further elaborated in Chapter 4. In this, the aim is to deliver services beyond the intrinsic objective of 'sport for its own sake' and more towards 'sport for the greater good' (Brookes & Wiggan, 2009). Participatory sporting events, such as running events, are increasingly associated with creating public value as they are thought to enhance public health through the promotion of physical activity, to contribute to social integration and to provide economic and social cohesion (Hover et al., 2016). Not only governments, but commercial as well as voluntary organisations, too, have to take up their social responsibility and have to add value to the public sphere reaching out beyond mere market economic logics (Bennington, 2011). It is remarkable, though, that in their efforts to create public value, providers from different profit sectors are increasingly dependent on each other. This is likely to be the case in regard to the organisation of running events as there seems to be an indispensable interplay between public, commercial and/or voluntary actors. For instance, to organise a city marathon, the city council needs both professionals and volunteers, hence the intensive collaboration with expert organisations from the commercial and the voluntary sectors. This is an appropriate example of how actors from different sectors (i.e., commercial, public and voluntary) can act in close partnership in the delivery of running services to a large audience.

For a long time, there was a clear distinction between the three sectors and what services were provided by which sector. However, overlaps occur as the distinction between different types of providers have become somewhat blurred. This implies that similar services (e.g., running programmes) or facilities (e.g., running accommodations) may be offered by more than one sector at the same time. Currently, as mentioned earlier, the provision of a running service or a running facility increasingly takes a mix of two or more partners from different sectors. This is especially the case when there seems to be a convergence of interests and objectives, among which is the promotion of physical activity. Such complementary partnerships are typical of the co-governance management model (Groeneveld, 2009; Skelcher, 2000). In this model, according to the so-called paradigm of 'networked community governance', coordination through networks and partnerships, as well as the process of co-creation across the different profit sectors, is central (Benington, 2011). This also applies to the world of sport, and the running industry in particular

(Scheerder et al., 2015b). Creating public value requires a wide and diverse network of different actors and institutions, as it cannot be created efficaciously by a single actor on its own. The involvement of more than one actor also leads to a more balanced governance structure, in which the respective strengths and assets of the different actors are respected, and, ideally, bundled. This is akin to the concept of a 'tripartite governance model', which can also be applied to (event) running (Eichberg, 2008; Scheerder et al., 2015b). In this multi-governing model, actors from different sectors are represented to ensure that a diversity of both public and private strategies and values is considered. Instead of sharp cleavages between different providers, non-hierarchical interrelationships with a variety of players are set up, resulting in a delivery of services and products that are accessible to many groups of sports consumers (Scheerder, 2020). In this way, it may also be expected that the needs and aspirations of current and potential segments of runners will be better met, and consequently that a better profit is assured from the health and social benefits recreational running offers.

Conclusions

At present, recreational running has a big following worldwide, as has been empirically demonstrated in this chapter, both by international surveys and country-specific data. More precisely, it has been shown that in the post-WWII period, three consecutive waves of recreational running can be discerned. The first and second running waves began at the end of the 1960s and at the end of 1990s, respectively. Based on fairly recent developments, namely festivalisation, extremisation and self-quantification, a third wave started to unfold. Along with these respective waves, recreational running has undergone profound changes, due to societal processes such as de-traditionalisation, de-sportification and informalisation, by (i) placing less emphasis on both formal and competitive aspects, (ii) realising a partial democratisation in terms of sex and age, and (iii) facilitating a 'scene-isation' of running as a result of the commodification and commercialisation processes. As such, an advanced running market was created, reaching out to billions of running participants. Still, running needs to enhance its appeal to wider sociodemographic groups as, to date, recreational running continues to mainly attract people with a rather higher social status. This would require a better understanding of how to promote running to various groups, which is discussed in Chapter 3, as well as the social and economic impacts of running events, as increasingly public support has been linked to demonstrating impacts, a topic that will be further explored in Chapter 4. Moreover, non-traditional forms of recreational running are on the rise, implying, among other things, that the market share of natural bodies, such as athletic clubs and their umbrella structures, further decreases as new and innovative running services and products are increasingly delivered by commercial providers. This is not to say, however, that there would be no longer a role left for civil society actors or for local and national governments. Within the framework of their public welfare policies, and Sport for All programmes in particular, public authorities as well as federations and clubs were at the basis of stimulating various forms of health-enhancing physical activities, especially recreational running. These institutions are still in a good position to add value to the public sphere by taking up their social responsibility. Yet, to create public value, it will be of uppermost concern that actors from all sectors, each with their own specific policy orientations and objectives, join forces, and in this way strive to meet the aspirations of distinct segments of (potential) runners.

Notes

1 We borrow the concept of 'eventscape' from Brown (2020) who defines an eventscape as a physical location, namely a place of local actors, but also a space of flows which make connections with external networks (Brown, 2020, p. 11).
2 The Run for Health project was granted by the European Commission. In the context of this project, several running events in different European countries were studied (see also Table 1.2 in Chapter 1). Two of those running events are the *AG Antwerp Ten Miles & Marathon* and the *Eindejaarscorrida Leuven*. For more details on these two events, we refer to the second case study of the present chapter.
3 According to the most recent ARRS data, in 2016, the daily average of marathons equals fourteen (authors' own calculation based on Milroy et al., 2018).
4 It is remarkable that the number of finishers as reported by Andersen and Nikolova (s.a.) refers to less than ten million finishers, in particular when we consider the numbers of finishers that we refer to in this chapter as well, as regard running events in countries like Belgium, Japan and the US (see Figures 2.3–2.5). We therefore suggest to interpret these absolute numbers with caution. However, the trend behind the results reported can be considered as indicative.
5 Only countries for which more than three ratios could be calculated are included.
6 In Italy, a social parity seemingly occurs. However, this exceptional position can be partly explained as the sample size was rather small and not controlled for representativeness (Helsen & Scheerder, 2020, p. 50).

References

Alexandris, K., Barkoukis, V., Karagiorgos, T., Ntovoli, A., de Brito, M., Middelkamp, E., Mitas, O., van Liere, L., Ahonen, A., Girginov, V., Di Tommaso, V., Moliterni, S., Ruggeri, A., Helsen, K., Scheerder, J., Kreivyte, R., Mejeryte-Narkeviciene, K., Valantine, I., Hover, P., van Eldert, P. (2021). *Promoting health enhancing physical activity and social welfare through outdoor running events* (RUN for HEALTH Project Reports). Thessaloniki: Aristotle University of Thessaloniki. https://runforhealth.eu/tools-materials/reports (accessed 20 November 2021).

Andersen, J.J. (2021). *The state of running 2019*. https://runrepeat.com/state-of-running (accessed 4 July 2022).

Andersen, J.J. & Nikolova, I. (s.a.). *The global state of running*. s.l.: IAAF/RunRepeat.

Atkinson, M. (2010). Fell running in post-sport territories. *Qualitative Research in Sport & Exercise*, 2(2): 109–132. DOI: 10.1080/19398441.2010.488020.

Atkinson, M. (2016). The suffering and loneliness of the fell runner. An ethnographic foray. In: G. Molnar & L. Purdy (Eds.). *Ethnographies in sport and exercise research* (pp. 96–110). London: Routledge.

Bale, J. (2004). *Running cultures. Racing in time and space*. London: Frank Cass.

Bennington, J. (2011). From private choice to public value. In: J. Bennington & M.H. Moore (Eds.). *Public value. Theory and practice*. (pp. 31–51). Basingstoke: Palgrave Macmillan.

Borgers, J., Vanreusel, B., Vos, S., Forsberg, P., & Scheerder, J. (2016). Do light sport facilities foster sports participation? A case study on the use of bark running tracks. *International Journal of Sport Policy & Politics*, 8(2): 287–304. DOI: 10.1080/19406940.2015.1116458.

Borgers, J., Vos, S., & Scheerder, J. (2015). Belgium (Flanders). Trends and governance in running. In: J. Scheerder, K. Breedveld & J. Borgers (Eds.). *Running across Europe. The rise and size of one of the largest sport markets*. (pp. 28–58). Basingstoke: Palgrave Macmillan.

Bourdieu, P. (1978). Sport and social class. *Social Science Information*, 17(6): 819–840.

Bourdieu, P. (1984). *Distinction. A social critique of the judgement of taste*. Cambridge, MA: Harvard University Press.

Breedveld, K., & Scheerder, J. (2017). The business of running. In: U. Wagner, R.K. Storm & K. Nielsen (Eds.). *When sport meets business. Capabilities, challenges, critiques*. (pp. 57–72). London: Sage.

Breedveld, K., Scheerder, J., & Borgers, J. (2015). Running across Europe. The way forward. In: J. Scheerder, K. Breedveld & J. Borgers (Eds.). *Running across Europe. The rise and size of one of the largest sport markets* (pp. 241–264). Basingstoke: Palgrave Macmillan.

Bridel, W., Markula, P., & Denison, J. (2016). Critical considerations of runners and running. In: W. Bridel, P. Markula & J. Denison (Eds.). *Endurance running. A socio-cultural examination* (Routledge Research in Sport, Culture & Society). (pp. 1–15). London: Routledge.

Brookes, S. & Wiggan, J. (2009). Reflecting the public value of sport. A game of two halves? *Public Management Review, 11*(4): 401–420. DOI: 10.1080/14719030902989490.

Brown, G. (2020). *Eventscapes. Transforming place, space and experiences.* London: Routledge.

Capsi, J., & Llopis-Goig, R. (2021). Understanding the expansion of running from a social practice theory perspective. A case study focused on the city of Valencia. *Sport in Society.* DOI: 10.1080/17430437.2021.1970139.

Carter, T.F. (2018). *On running and becoming human. An anthropological perspective.* Cham: Springer.

Couture, J. (2021). Reflections from the 'Strava-sphere'. Kudos, community, and *(self-)surveillance on a social network for athletes. Qualitative Research in Sport, Exercise & Health, 13(1): 184–200. DOI: 10.1080/2159676X.2020.1836514.*

Crum, B. (1993). The sportification of the society and the internal differentiation of sport. In: EASM (Ed.). *Proceedings of the first European congress on sport management* (1st EASM Congress; Groningen; September 1993). (pp. 149–153). Groningen: European Association of Sport Management.

Egan-Wyer, C. (2019). *The sellable self. Exploring endurance running as an extraordinary consumption experience* (Lund Studies in Economics & Management 146). Lund: Lund University/School of Economics & Management.

Egan-Wyer, C. (2023). Neoliberal meanings of endurance experiences. A critical exploration of endurance running in contemporary consumer culture. In: N.B. Salazar & J. Scheerder (Eds.). *Contemporary meanings of endurance. An interdisciplinary approach* (Routledge Studies in Resilience) (pp. 98–119). London: Routledge.

Eichberg, H. (2008). *Pyramid or democracy in sports? Alternative ways in European sports policies.* www.idrottsforum.org/articles/eichberg/eichberg 080206.pdf (accessed 12 July 2022).

Elmose-Østerlund, K., Ibsen, B., Nagel, S., & Scheerder, J. (2020). The contribution of sports clubs to public welfare in European societies. A cross-national comparative perspective. In: S. Nagel, K. Elmose-Østerlund, B. Ibsen & J. Scheerder (Eds.). *Functions of sports clubs in European societies. A cross-national comparative study* (Sports Economics, Management & Policy 13). (pp. 345–385). Cham: Springer.

Florida, R. (2012). *The rise of the creative class, revisited.* New York, NY: Basic.

Funk, D.C., Alexandris, K., & McDonald, H. (Eds.) (2016). *Sport consumer behaviour. Marketing strategies.* London: Routledge.

Grant, R.R., & Teahan, B. (2019). Pricing footraces in the United States. An application of hedonic pricing to the running industry. *The American Economist, 64*(2): 293–305. DOI: 10.1177/0569434519841037.

Groeneveld, M. (2009). European sport governance, citizens and the state. Finding a (co-)productive balance for the twenty-first century. *Public Management Review, 11*(4): 421–440. DOI: 10.1080/14719030902989516.

Heelas, P. (1996). Introduction. Detraditionalization and its rivals. In: P. Heelas, S. Lash & P. Morris (Eds.). *Detraditionalization. Critical reflections on authority and identity.* (pp. 1–20). Oxford: Blackwell.

Helsen, K., Derom, I., Corthouts, J., De Bosscher, V., Willem, A., & Scheerder, J. (2021). Participatory sport events in times of COVID-19. Analysing the (virtual) sport behaviour of event participants (Special Issue on Sport and COVID-19: Impact and Challenges for the Future). *European Sport Management Quarterly, 21*(2). DOI: 10.1080/16184742.2021.1956560.

Helsen, K., Janssen, M., Vos, S., & Scheerder, J. (2022). Two of a kind? Similarities and differences between runners and walkers in sociodemographic characteristics, sports related characteristics and wearable usage. *International Journal of Environmental Research & Public Health 19*(15). DOI: 10.3390/ijerph19159284.

Helsen, K., & Scheerder, J., with the cooperation of Alexandris, K. & Hover, P. (2020). *Flemish running events in international perspective. Participant profile, motivation and attitudes. Results based on the European RUN for HEALTH project* (Sport Policy & Management Studies 72). Leuven: KU Leuven/Policy in Sports & Physical Activity Research Group. https://gbiomed.kuleuven.be/english/research/50000737/groups/policy-in-sports-physical-activity-research-group/spm-studies/copy_of_bms72-spm.pdf (accessed 7 July 2022).

Helsen, K., & Scheerder, J., with the cooperation of Vos, S., Salazar, N., Lanclus, E., Könecke, T., Hugaerts, I., & Thibaut, E. (2022). *De Vlaamse loop- en wandelsporter in beeld. Leuven Running & Walking Study2.0 (LRWS2.0): resultaten van de loopsporters (deel 2)* [The Flemish running and walking participant in figures. Leuven Running & Walking Study2.0 (LRWS2.0): results concerning the runners (part 2)] (Sport Policy & Management Studies 111). Leuven: KU Leuven/Policy in Sports & Physical Activity Research Group. https://gbiomed.kuleuven.be/english/research/50000737/groups/policy-in-sports-physical-activity-research-group/bms-studies/studies/bms111.pdf (accessed 13 July 2022).

Helsen, K., Scheerder, J., Girginov, V., & Ahonen, A. (2020). *Policy recommendations to promote health-enhancing physical activity and social welfare in the EU. Results based on the European RUN for HEALTH project* (Sport Policy & Management Studies 75). Leuven: KU Leuven/Policy in Sports & Physical Activity Research Group. https://gbiomed.kuleuven.be/english/research/50000737/groups/policy-in-sports-physical-activity-research-group/spm-studies/copy_of_bms75-spm.pdf (accessed 12 July 2022).

Hoekman, R., Van der Werff, H., Nagel, S., & Breuer, C. (2015). A cross-national comparative perspective on sport clubs in Europe. In: C. Breuer, R. Hoekman, S. Nagel & H. Van der Werff (Eds.). *Sport clubs in Europe. A cross-national comparative perspective* (Sports Economics, Management & Policy 12). (pp. 419–435). Cham: Springer.

Hover, P. (2013). Derde loopgolf dient zich aan [The third wave of running is knocking at the door]. www.sportnext.nl/beleid/derde-loopgolf-dient-zich-aan/ (accessed 19 June 2022).

Hover, P., Dijk, B., Breedveld, K., & Van Eekeren, F. (2016). *Integrity & sport events* (Position paper). Utrecht: Mulier Institute & Utrecht University.

Hover, P., Van der Werff, H. & Breedveld, K. (2015). The Netherlands. Rising participation rates, shifting segments. In: J. Scheerder, K. Breedveld &

J. Borgers (Eds.). *Running across Europe. The rise and size of one of the largest sport markets.* (pp. 187–207). Basingstoke: Palgrave Macmillan.

Janssen, M. (2022). Understanding recreational runners' motives and behaviour to support the design of running-related technology (published doctoral thesis). Eindhoven: Eindhoven University of Technology.

Janssen, M., Scheerder, J., Thibaut, E., Brombacher, A., & Vos, S. (2017). Who uses running apps and sports watches? Determinants and consumer profiles of event runners' usage of running-related smartphone applications and sports watches. *PLoS One, 12*(7): e0181167. DOI: 10.1371/journal.pone.0181167.

Janssen, M., Walravens, R., Thibaut, E., Scheerder, J., Brombacher, A., & Vos, S. (2020). Understanding different types of recreational runners and how they use running-related technology. *International Journal of Environmental Research & Public Health, 17*(7). DOI: 10.3390/ijerph17072276.

Knippenberg, J. (1987). *De mens als duurloper* [Man as long-distance runner]. Rijswijk: Elmar Sport.

Kurtoglu-Hooton, N. (2021). *Language, identity online and running.* Cham: Palgrave Macmillan.

Lanclus, E. (2023). Unpacking contemporary notions of endurance through the lens of ultra-trail running and walking. In: N.B. Salazar & J. Scheerder (Eds.). *Contemporary meanings of endurance. An interdisciplinary approach* (Routledge Studies in Resilience) (pp. 120–138). London: Routledge.

Llopis-Goig, R. (2014). Sports participation and cultural trends. Running as a reflection of individualization and post-materialism processes in Spanish society. *European Journal for Sport & Society, 11*(2): 151–169. DOI: 10.1080/16138171.2014.11687938.

McGehee, N.G., Yoon, Y., & Cardenas, D. (2003). Involvement and travel for recreational runners in North Carolina. *Journal of Sport Management, 17*(3): 305–324. DOI: 10.1123/jsm.17.3.305.

McKay, T., McEwan, L., & Baker, M. (2019). The rise of trail running in South Africa. Possibilities for small-scale sports tourism. *GeoJournal of Tourism & Geosites, 26*(3): 930–942. DOI: 10.30892/gtg.26320-408.

Milroy, A., Gasparovic, J., Post, M., & Peckiconis, S. (2018). *The future of the ARRS.* www.arrs.run (accessed 4 July 2022).

Murakami, H. (2008). *What I talk about when I talk about running. A memoir.* New York, NY: Alfred A. Knopf.

Patty, J.A. (2016). Running, the people's sport. In: D.C. Funk, K. Alexandris & H. McDonald (Eds.). *Sport consumer behaviour. Marketing strategies.* (pp. 306–310). London: Routledge.

Pine, B.J., & Gilmore, J.H. (1999). *The experience economy. Work is theatre and every business a stage.* Boston, MA: Harvard Business School Press.

Rauter, S., & Topic, M.D. (2014). Runners as sport tourists. The experience and travel behaviors of Ljubljana Marathon participants. *Collegium Antropologicum, 38*(3): 909–915.

Renson, R. (1976). Social status symbolism of sports stratification. *Hermes* (Leuven), *10*: 433–443.

Rizzo, N. (2021). *120+ running statistics 2021/2022* (research review). https://runrepeat.com/running-statistics (accessed 10 July 2022).
Ronto, P. (2021). *The state of ultra running 2020.* https://runrepeat.com/state-of-ultra-running (accessed 11 July 2022).
Running USA (2020). *U.S. running trends.* www.wpr.org/sites/default/files/-running_usa_trends_report_2019-r4.pdf (accessed 10 July 2022).
Salazar, N.B., & Scheerder, J. (2023). Endurance as an analytical concept and a lived experience. A transdisciplinary exploration. In: N.B. Salazar & J. Scheerder (Eds.). *Contemporary meanings of endurance. An interdisciplinary approach* (Routledge Studies in Resilience) (pp. 1–8). London: Routledge.
Sánchez García, R. (2019). Informalisation and sport. The case of jogging/running in the USA (1960–2000). In: C. Wouters & M. Dunning (Eds.). *Civilisation and informalisation. Connecting long-term social and psychic processes.* (pp. 247–266). Cham: Springer.
Scheerder, J. (2007). *Tofsport in Vlaanderen. Groei, omvang en segmentatie van de Vlaamse recreatiesportmarkt* [Recreational sport in Flanders. Growth, size and segmentation of the Flemish Sport for All market]. Antwerp: F&G Partners.
Scheerder, J. (2017). *Running for all and all for running. A focus on trends and demographics* (Keynote presented at the 1st European Running Business Conference; Frankfurt; October 27–28, 2017).
Scheerder, J. (2020). Established models of European sport revisited from a socio-politological approach. In: N.R. Porro, S. Martelli & A. Testa (Eds.). *Sport, welfare and social policy in the European Union* (Routledge Research in Sport, Culture & Society). (pp. 153–168). London: Routledge.
Scheerder, J., & Boen, F. (Eds.) (2009). *Vlaanderen loopt! Sociaalwetenschappelijk onderzoek naar de loopsportmarkt* [Mass participation running in Flanders. Social scientific research of the running market] (SBS Studies 1). Ghent: Academia Press.
Scheerder, J., & Breedveld, K. (2013). *The running landscape of Europe. Why is running growing so fast?* (Keynote presented at the 8th Play the Game Conference 'Stepping up for democracy in sport'; Aarhus, October 28–31, 2013).
Scheerder, J., Breedveld, K., & Borgers, J. (Eds.) (2015a). *Running across Europe. The rise and size of one of the largest sport markets.* Basingstoke: Palgrave Macmillan.
Scheerder, J., Breedveld, K., & Borgers, J. (2015b). Who is doing a run with the running boom? The growth and governance of one of Europe's most popular sport activities. In: J. Scheerder, K. Breedveld & J. Borgers (Eds.). *Running across Europe. The rise and size of one of the largest sport markets.* (pp. 1–27). Basingstoke: Palgrave Macmillan.
Scheerder, J., & Thibaut, E. (2021a). *Flemish Household Study on Sports Participation 2019. Social status pyramid of sports participation in Flanders according to socio-professional status* (Sport Policy & Management Infographics 106). Leuven: KU Leuven/Policy in Sports & Physical Activity Research Group. https://gbiomed.kuleuven.be/english/research/50000737/groups/policy-in-sports-physical-activity-research-group/spm-studies/copy_of_spm-infographic-piramide-20211213.pdf (accessed 7 July 2022).

Scheerder, J., & Thibaut, E. (2021b). *Studie over de Bewegingsactiviteiten in Vlaanderen (SBV) 1969–2019. De sociale gelaagdheid van sportbeoefening* [Study on physical activities in Flanders 1969–2019. The social stratification of sport participation] (Beleid & Management in Sport Studies 101). Leuven: KU Leuven/Policy in Sports & Physical Activity Research Group. https://gbiomed.kuleuven.be/english/research/50000737/groups/policy-in-sports-physical-activity-research-group/bms-studies/studies/bms101-finaal.pdf (accessed 7 July 2022).

Scheerder, J., & Thibaut, E. (2021c). *Studie over de Bewegingsactiviteiten in Vlaanderen (SBV) 1969–2019. Een halve eeuw sportparticipatie in cijfers* [Study on physical activities in Flanders 1969–2019. Half a century of sports participation in figures] (Beleid & Management in Sport Studies 100). Leuven: KU Leuven/Policy in Sports & Physical Activity Research Group. https://gbiomed.kuleuven.be/english/research/50000737/groups/policy-in-sports-physical-activity-research-group/bms-studies/studies/bms100-finaal.pdf (accessed 7 July 2022).

Scheerder, J., Vandermeerschen, H., Van Tuyckom, C., Hoekman, R., Breedveld, K., & Vos, S. (2011). *Understanding the game: sport participation in Europe. Facts, reflections and recommendations* (Sport Policy & Management Studies 10). Leuven: KU Leuven/Research Unit of Social Kinesiology & Sport Management. https://gbiomed.kuleuven.be/english/research/50000737/groups/policy-in-sports-physical-activity-research-group/spm-studies/bms10-spm.pdf (accessed 7 July 2022).

Scheerder, J., Vanreusel, B., Taks, M., & Renson, R. (2002). Social sports stratification in Flanders 1969–1999. Intergenerational reproduction of social inequalities? *International Review for the Sociology of Sport, 37*(2): 219–245. DOI: 10.1177/1012690202037002006.

Sillitoe, A. (1959). *The loneliness of the long-distance runner and other stories.* London: W.H. Allen.

Skelcher, C. (2000). Changing images of the state. Overloaded, hollowed-out, congested. *Public Policy & Administration, 15*(3): 3–19. DOI: 10.1177/095207670001500302.

Smith, S.L. (1998). Athletes, runners and joggers. Participant-group dynamics in a sport of 'individuals'. *Sociology of Sport Journal, 15*(2): 174–192. DOI: 10.1123/ssj.15.2.174.

Söderberg, M. (2014). Willingness to pay for nontraditional attributes among participants of a long-distance running race. *Journal of Sports Economics, 15*(3): 285–302. DOI: 10.1177/1527002512452876.

Stokvis, R. (2005). De popularisering van het hardlopen [Popularisation of running]. *Sociologie, 2*(3): 249–264.

Strava (2020). *Year in sport 2020.* https://1n4rcn88bk4ziht713dla5ub-wpengine.netdna-ssl.com/wp-content/uploads/2020/12/UK_YIS_2020.pdf (accessed 4 July 2022).

Thibaut, E., Constandt, B., De Bosscher, V., Willem, A., Ricour, M., & Scheerder, J. (2021a). Sports participation during lockdown. How COVID-19 changed the sports frequency and motivation of participants in club, event, and online sports. *Leisure Studies, 41*(4): 457-470. DOI: 10.1080/02614367.2021.2014941.

Thibaut, E., Vos, S., & Scheerder, J. (2021b). Running apparel consumption explained. A diary approach. *Journal of Global Sport Management, 6*(4): 373–387. DOI: 10.1080/24704067.2019.1639064.

Van Bottenburg, M. (2006). A second wave of running? *Sport Marketing Europe, 1*(1): 26–30.

Van Bottenburg, M., Rijnen, B., & Sterkenburg, J. (2005). *Sports participation in the European Union. Trends and differences.* Nieuwegein: Arko Sports Media.

Van Bottenburg, M., Scheerder, J., & Hover, P. (2010). Don't miss the next boat. Europe's opportunities and challenges in the second wave of running. *New Studies in Athletics, 25*(3/4): 125–143.

Van Dyck, D., Cardon, G., De Bourdeaudhuij, I., De Ridder, L., & Willem, A. (2017). Who participates in running events? Socio-demographic characteristics, psychosocial factors and barriers as correlates of non-participation. A pilot study in Belgium. *International Journal of Environmental Research & Public Health, 14*(11). DOI: 10.3390/ijerph14111315.

Vanreusel, B. (1984). Running as a mass movement. In: Société Française de Sociologie du Sport (Ed.). *Sport et sociétés contemporaines* (8th Symposium of the International Committee for Sociology of Sport; Institut National du Sport & de l'Education Physique, Paris, 6–10 July 1983). (pp. 601–608). Paris: Société Française de Sociologie du Sport.

Vanreusel, B., & Taks, M. (1998). Sport for All? A critical appraisal of 25 years of sport democratization. In: ISA (Ed.). *Sociological knowledge, heritage, challenges, perspectives* (Book of abstracts of the 14th Congrès Mondial de Sociologie; Montréal, 26 July – 1 August). (p. 393). Montréal: International Sociology Association.

Wearing, B., & Wearing, S. (1992). Identity and the commodification of leisure. *Leisure Studies, 11*(1): 3–18. DOI: 10.1080/02614369100390271.

Weedon, G. (2016). On the entangled origins of mud running. "Overcivilization," physical culture, and overcoming obstacles in the Spartan Race. In: W. Bridel, P. Markula & J. Denison (Eds.). *Endurance running. A sociocultural examination* (Routledge Research in Sport, Culture & Society). (pp. 35–49). London: Routledge.

Wicker, P., & Hallmann, K. (2013). Estimating consumer's willingness-to-pay for participation in and travelling to marathon events. *Event Management, 17*: 271–282. DOI: 10.3727/152599513X13708863377953.

Wouters, C. (2007). *Informalization. Manners and emotions since 1890.* London: Sage.

Case study 2.1 The AG Antwerp Ten Miles & Marathon and the Brussels 20 km Race Trends in Participant Numbers and Profiles

Kobe Helsen and Jeroen Scheerder

Running has traditionally been a very popular sport in Flanders (Belgium), both among youngsters and adults (Borgers et al., 2015; Scheerder et al., 2013; Scheerder & Thibaut, 2021). Running can be practised in a variety of organisational contexts (such as athletics clubs or running clubs), but in non-organised contexts as well (such as light running communities, unorganised with friends or alone; Borgers et al., 2015). This case study analyses the trends as regards the number of participants and changes in participant profiles (e.g., sex, age and finish times of event participants) of the two largest running events in Flanders: the AG Antwerp Ten Miles & Marathon and the Brussels 20 km race (*20 km door Brussel*). Both events were initiated in the eighties, and thus have experienced a remarkable evolution (see also Alexandris et al., 2021).

The AG Antwerp Ten Miles & Marathon is an event that offers different distances: a short run (5 to 6 km, this varies each edition), a ladies' run (5–6 km for ladies only, this varies each edition), a 10 miles run (16 km) and a marathon (42 km). Not all distances were offered in each edition of the event. The short run was added to the programme from 2004 onwards and the ladies run from 2006 onwards (also in 2003, there was a specific lady run). The marathon was combined with the 10 miles run as of 2007. The ladies run was removed from the programme in 2017. The marathon was removed from the programme in 2021 and was transformed into a new event at a different place in the calendar (September). The Brussels 20 km race solely offers a 20 km run and in 2021 a race for walkers was added. In 2019, around 700 running events were organised in Flanders (Helsen & Scheerder, 2020). The Brussels 20 km race and AG Antwerp Ten Miles & Marathon were the largest running events by far (with around 30,000 participants in 2019; see Figure 2.9), with the third biggest Flemish running event being three times smaller.

Events participation numbers

Nurtured by, among others, trends like the fitness revolution, democratisation, and commercialisation, the number of running events grew in Flanders (Borgers et al., 2015; Helsen & Scheerder, 2020) as well as worldwide (see Chapter 2 and Scheerder et al., 2015) in the past decennia. As a result, the number of people participating in running events increased as well. Figure 2.9 shows the number of participants in the Brussels 20 km race and AG Antwerp Ten Miles & Marathon between 1980 and 2022.[1] Figure 1 shows the increase before 1985 as regards the Brussels 20 km race denoting the end of the first running wave. After a stagnation in the 1990s, a second running wave started around the new millennium as can be seen in Figure 2.9. The popularity of both events skyrocketed, reaching the highest participation numbers in 2014, but stagnated from 2017. Due to COVID-19, the 2020 edition of both events was cancelled (however, people were able to virtually run the AG Antwerp Ten Miles & Marathon in 2020). The 2021 edition of both events attracted significantly less participants for different reasons. First of all, there were COVID-19 measures and there was an organisational uncertainty for the event organisers. Second, the events

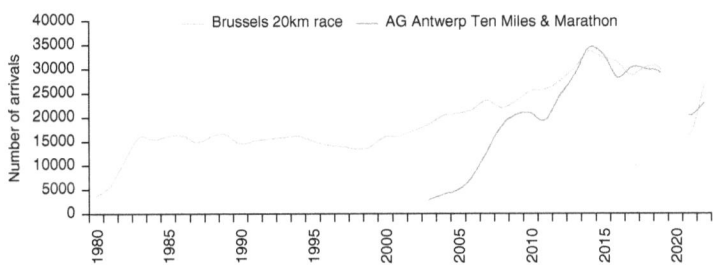

Figure 2.9 Number of finishers at the AG Antwerp Ten Miles & Marathon and the Brussels 20 km race (1980–2022).

Source: Adapted by authors' own calculations from www.acn-timing.com; www.assaronse.be; www.chronorace.be; www.stratenlopen.be and Scheerder and Noppe (2009).

Note. No data were available for the AG Antwerp Ten Miles & Marathon before 2003. Due to COVID-19, the 2020 editions of both running events were cancelled. In 2021 and 2022, the marathon distance of the AG Antwerp Ten Miles & Marathon was removed from the programme to launch a new event at a different time in the season. Therefore, the name of the event was changed to 'AG Antwerp Ten Miles'. The 2021 editions were organised in the fall instead of the spring. There was a participant limit for the AG Antwerp Ten Miles & Marathon in 2021. The Brussels 20 km race offered both a physical and a virtual (not included in the figure) event in 2021 and introduced the category of walkers to the programme.

were organised in the fall instead of the traditional dates in the spring. Third, a participant limit was set for the AG Antwerp Ten Miles & Marathon. Fourth, the marathon distance was removed from the programme for the AG Antwerp Ten Miles & Marathon. Lastly, the organisers of the Brussels 20 km race offered both a virtual and physical event in 2021 (virtual participation numbers are not included in the figure). Some people might have preferred to participate virtually instead of physically, for example, for fear of infection with COVID-19. Figure 2.10 shows the respective popularity of the different distances of the AG Antwerp Ten Miles & Marathon. Mainly, the short run distance and 10 miles distance show an increase in popularity from 2004 onwards.

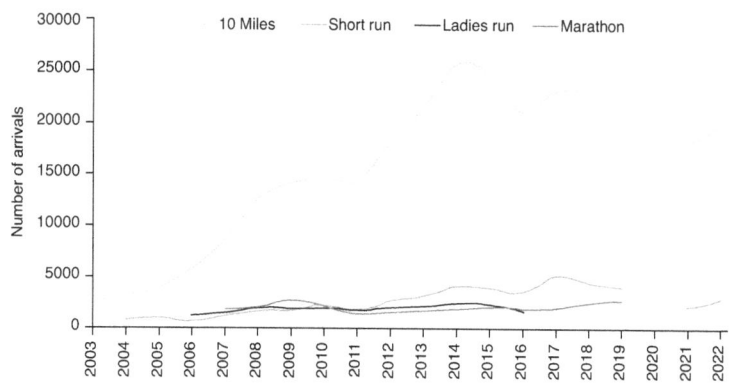

Figure 2.10 Number of finishers at the AG Antwerp Ten Miles & Marathon, according to different distances that were offered (2003–2022).

Source: Adapted by authors' own calculations from www.acn-timing.com; www.assaronse.be; www.chronorace.be; www.stratenlopen.be and Scheerder and Noppe (2009).

Note. No data were available for the AG Antwerp Ten Miles & Marathon before 2003. Due to COVID-19, the 2020 edition was cancelled. In 2017, the ladies run was removed from the programme. From 2021 onwards, the marathon distance of the AG Antwerp Ten Miles & Marathon was removed from the programme to launch a new event at a different time in the season. Therefore, the name of the event was changed to 'AG Antwerp Ten Miles'. The 2021 edition was organised in the fall instead of the spring. There was a participant limit for the 2021 edition.

Participants demographics: sex and age

The profile of participants in running events is more diverse than ever (Hallmann & Wicker, 2012; Janssen et al., 2020; Parra-Camacho et al., 2019; Scheerder et al., 2015). In 2004, 15% of participants in the Brussels 20 km race were foreigners (Scheerder & Noppe, 2009). This number increased to almost one-fifth of participants (19.8%) in 2018 and over one-fifth of participants (21.2%) in 2022 (authors' own calculations). In addition, the number of female participants has increased as well (mainly from the new millennium onwards). The number of female finishers participating in the Brussels 20 km race increased from 13.4% in 1984 to 35.5% in 2022 (see Table 2.3).

Contrary to the general ageing trend of running event participants (see Chapter 2), Table 2.4 shows that participants of the AG Antwerp Ten Miles & Marathon and Brussels 20 km race are

Table 2.3 Evolution of the number of female finishers at the Brussels 20 km race (1984–2022), in percentages

1984	1998	2003	2008	2013	2019	2022
13.4	14.4	17.7	24.2	26.3	31.4	35.5

Source: Adapted by authors' own calculations from www.assaronse.be; www.chronorarce.be; www.stratenlopen.be and Scheerder and Noppe (2009).

Table 2.4 Average age of finishers at two popular Flemish running events (between 2010 and 2019)

	AG Antwerp Ten Miles & Marathon		Brussels 20 km race	
	2012	2019	2010	2017
Total	36.0	35.5	Total 38.7	38.1
Ladies run	31.1	–		
Short run	28.1	28.1		
10 miles	37.1	36.3		
Marathon	41.9	40.1		

Source: Adapted by authors' own calculations from www.acn-timing.com; www.assaronse.be; www.chronorace.be; www.stratenlopen.be and Scheerder and Noppe (2009).

Note. The last edition of the Ladies run of the AG Antwerp Ten Miles & Marathon was held in 2016.

not getting older (over a seven-year period). On average, the participants of the AG Antwerp Ten Miles & Marathon are younger than those of the Brussels 20 km race (35.5 years vs. 38.1 years). The participants of both running events are younger than the overall average of running event participants worldwide of 39 years (Andersen, 2019; Galic, 2022; see also Chapter 2).

Finish times of participants

The increase in popularity of running in the past decades can be mainly attributed to the rise of the recreational runner rather than to the rise of the competitive runner. This can partly be explained by the processes of gender and age democratisation (i.e., a higher number of women and people of all ages participate), informalisation, commercialisation, etc. (Scheerder et al., 2015). People participate less for competitive and achievement reasons but rather for the social experiences and camaraderie. This caused an increase in the finish times at running events. Figures 2.11 and 2.12 show that, for the Brussels 20 km race and AG Antwerp Ten Miles & Marathon, respectively, people use more time to complete the distances (represented by a longer right tale for the more recent editions). In addition, the average time of the largest group of participants increases as well (the peak of the curves of the more recent editions moves to the right).

Take home messages

Based on the foregoing, two take home messages can be given for stakeholders in the running event industry.

a   Running is a very popular leisure-time activity and in the past decades the profile of running event participants diversified. Event organisers should respond to this trend of changing profiles and at the same time should consider possible target groups that are not yet reached. This can be done by organising running events with different formats or purposes, by offering different formats within one event, or by organising auxiliary events, however, without passing by the event concept (see also Chapter 3).

The running eventscape 55

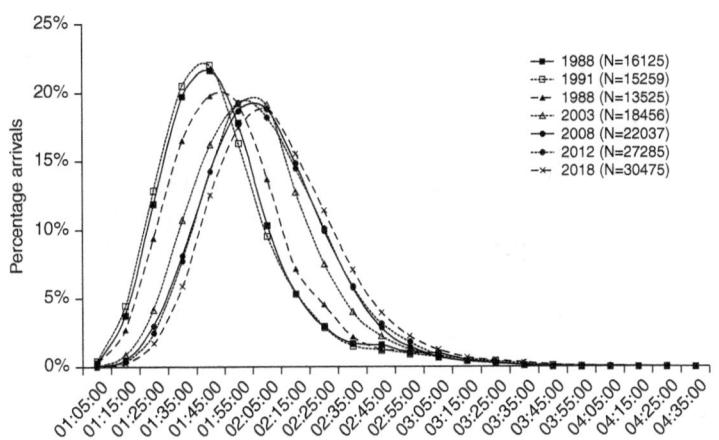

Figure 2.11 Evolution of finishing times at the Brussels 20 km race (1988–2018).
Source: Adapted by authors' own calculations from www.assaronse.be; www.chronorace.be; www.stratenlopen.be and Scheerder and Noppe (2009).

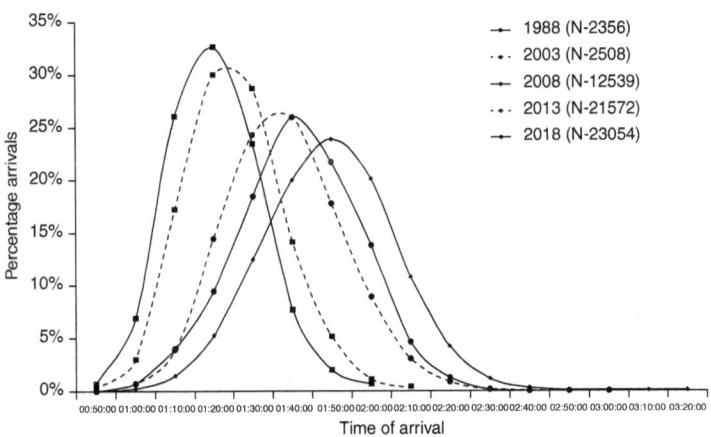

Figure 2.12 Evolution of finishing times at the AG Antwerp Ten Miles & Marathon (1988–2018).
Source: Adapted by authors' own calculations from www.acn-timing.com; www.assaronse.be; www.chronorace.be; www.stratenlopen.be and Scheerder and Noppe (2009).

b In general, social experiences are getting more important during running events. Event organisers should respond to wishes of participants by including related activities to enhance the atmosphere. Event organisers can also go a step further by creating a whole customer journey (that starts by subscribing for the event and ends when the participant arrives home after the event). Of course, there still remains a group of people who solely focus on competition and achievement. Therefore, there should remain a permanent offer for this group of participants (see also 'Market segmentation' in Chapter 3).

Note

1 Unfortunately, no data were available for the AG Antwerp Ten Miles & Marathon before 2003.

References

Alexandris, K., Barkoukis, V., Karagiorgos, T., Ntovoli, A., de Brito, M., Middelkamp, E., Mitas, O., van Liere, L., Ahonen, A., Girginov, V., Di Tommaso, V., Moliterni, S., Ruggeri, A., Helsen, K., Scheerder, J., Kreivyte, R., Mejeryte-Narkeviciene, K., Valantine, I., Hover, P., & van Eldert, P. (2021). *Promoting health enhancing physical activity and social welfare through outdoor running events. Case studies report* (RUN for HEALTH Project Report 5). Thessaloniki: Aristotle University of Thessaloniki.

Andersen, J.J. (2019). *The state of running 2019.* https://racemedicine.org/the-state-of-running-2019/ (accessed 13 April 2022).

Borgers, J., Vos, S., & Scheerder, J. (2015). Belgium (Flanders). Trends and governance in running. In: J. Scheerder, K. Breedveld & J. Borgers (Eds.). *Running across Europe. The rise and size of one of the largest sport markets.* (pp. 28–58). Basingstoke: Palgrave Macmillan.

Galic, B. (2022). 126 Running statistics you need to know. https://www.livestrong.com/article/13730338-running-statistics/ (accessed 13 April 2022).

Hallmann, K., & Wicker, P. (2012). Consumer profiles of runners at marathon races. *International Journal of Event & Festival Management, 3*: 171–187.

Helsen, K., & Scheerder, J., with the cooperation of Alexandris, K., & Hover, P. (2020). *Flemish running events in international perspective: Participant profile, motivation and attitudes. Results based* on the European RUN for HEALTH project (Sport Policy & Management Studies 72). Leuven: KU Leuven/Policy in Sports & Physical Activity Research Group. https://gbiomed.kuleuven.be/english/research/50000737/groups/policy-in-sports-physical-activity-research-group/spm-studies/copy_of_bms72-spm.pdf (accessed 7 July 2022).

Janssen, M., Walravens, R., Thibaut, E., Scheerder, J., Brombacher, A., & Vos, S. (2020). Understanding different types of recreational runners and how they use running-related technology. *International Journal of Environmental Research & Public Health, 17*(7). DOI: 10.3390/ijerph17072276.

Parra-Camacho, D., González-Serrano, M.H., González-García, R.J., & Moreno, F.C. (2019). Sporting habits of urban runners: Classification according to their motivation. *International Journal of Environmental Research & Public Health, 16*(24). DOI: 10.3390/ijerph16244990.

Scheerder, J., Breedveld, K., & Borgers, J. (2015). Who is doing a run with the running boom? The growth and governance of one of Europe's most popular sport activities. In: J. Scheerder, K. Breedveld & J. Borgers (Eds.). *Running across Europe. The rise and size of one of the largest sport markets.* (pp. 1–27). Basingstoke: Palgrave Macmillan.

Scheerder, J., & Noppe, L. (2009). Local running: Ontwikkelingen en potentiële groei van de loopsportparticipatie in Vlaanderen [Local running: Developments and potential growth of running participation in Flanders]. In: J. Scheerder & F. Boen (Eds.). *Vlaanderen loopt! Sociaal-wetenschappelijk onderzoek naar de loopsportmarkt* [Mass participation running in Flanders. Social scientific research of the running market] (SBS Studies 1). (pp. 79–124). Ghent: Academia Press.

Scheerder, J., & Thibaut, E. (2021c). *Studie over de Bewegingsactiviteiten in Vlaanderen (SBV) 1969–2019. Een halve eeuw sportparticipatie in cijfers* [Study on physical activities in Flanders 1969–2019. Half a century of sports participation in figures] (Beleid & Management in Sport Studies 100). Leuven: KU Leuven/Policy in Sports & Physical Activity Research Group. https://gbiomed.kuleuven.be/english/research/50000737/groups/policy-in-sports-physical-activity-research-group/bms-studies/studies/bms100-finaal.pdf (accessed 7 July 2022).

Scheerder, J., Vandermeerschen, H., Borgers, J., Thibaut, E., & Vos, S. (2013). *Vlaanderen sport! Vier decennia sportbeleid en sportparticipatie* [Flanders sports active! Four decades of sports policy and sports participation] (SBS Studies 5). Ghent: Academia Press.

Case study 2.2 The AG Antwerp Ten Miles & Marathon and the Eindejaarscorrida Leuven Comparing Events Policy, Events Marketing and Events Impact Between a Commercial and Voluntary Running Event Provider

Kobe Helsen and Jeroen Scheerder

The AG Antwerp Ten Miles & Marathon and the Eindejaarscorrida Leuven were initiated in the past millennium (1980 for the marathon and 1986 for the Ten Miles as regards the former, 1997 as regards the latter; see Alexandris et al., 2021). The AG Antwerp Ten Miles & Marathon is organised by a commercial event organiser (profit oriented; Golazo Sports), whereas the Eindejaarscorrida Leuven is organised by the local athletics club (not-for-profit oriented; Daring Club Leuven Atletiek). Both event organisers are extensively supported (both financially and logistically) by the local governments where the events are organised (respectively, Antwerp and Leuven). In the 2019 edition, 6,033 individuals participated in the Eindejaarscorrida Leuven of which 22% in the 4K run, 38% in the 8K run and 40% in the 12K run. 29,230 individuals participated in the AG Antwerp Ten Miles & Marathon of which 14% in the 5K run, 77% in the 10 miles run and 9% in the marathon (Helsen & Scheerder, 2020a; 2020b). In this case study, both events are studied as regards their policy (objectives), marketing and management, and impact.

Events policy

The policy of the two Flemish running events are discussed according to the extent to which the organisers deal with aspects of economic returns, sports-related returns, and city marketing. These three facets were, after all, deliberately cited as event objectives by the different event organisers and thus allow to make a discerning comparison (Alexandris et al., 2021).

The AG Antwerp Ten Miles & Marathon (henceforth Ten Miles) is a profitable running event. After all, the organiser of the event, Golazo Sports, is a profit-oriented organisation which needs a positive financial return to pay salary for staff and to invest in the further growth of the company. This return is realised by inscription fees of the many participants on the one hand,

and strategic implementation of sponsor packages (see further) as well as an elaborated business village[1] on the other hand. In contrast, the Eindejaarscorrida Leuven (henceforth Corrida) is not a profitable running event at all. If the organiser of the event, DCLA,[2] did not receive subsidies from the city over the past three years, they would have made a loss.

By organising the Corrida, the purpose of DCLA is to share their running culture to the public. For the organiser, attracting people to the club is not the main objective. In addition, they rarely notice an increase in the number of members before or after the event. The city of Leuven, as partner of the Corrida and local administration, does try to make the connection between other existing initiatives and the event in order to make residents (more) active. The city of Antwerp pursues this connection between existing initiatives and the Ten Miles as well, by supporting distinct running events with different distances throughout the year so that residents can move from one (running) event to another. Golazo Sports, as the main organiser of the Ten Miles, has a goal to get everyone moving for at least 30 minutes every day, by offering participatory (and spectator) sports events. They propose cities to not only invest in the event itself, but in a platform for participants to download training schedules too. Specifically for the Ten Miles, Golazo Sports works together with AG Insurance which is an insurance company (and name sponsor for the event). The company initiated an activation programme to promote active sports and a healthy lifestyle. Both cities of Antwerp and Leuven use the events for city marketing. The events are extensively covered in the news and have strong media partners.

To sum up, Golazo Sports and the city of Antwerp strive to organise the biggest running event in the country and both the organiser and participants work towards this important day (being the last Sunday of April and the unofficial start of running season). It is one of the largest annual participatory sports events for the two parties, which illustrates the collective governance model discussed in this chapter. Therefore, Golazo Sports receives extensive support from the city to ensure that everything runs as smoothly as possible (during the event and in the preparatory phases). In contrast, the Corrida is featured as a smaller-scale event. However, the event is cherished within the city as it is the largest local running event. In line with the city's image and the event's place in the calendar (between Christmas and New Year's Eve), the cosiness, convivial atmosphere, and small-scale setup remain emphasised.

Events marketing and management

The marketing and management of the two Flemish running events are discussed by focusing on the means of communication, the organisation of side events, the cost of participation, securing sponsors and the attractiveness of the event course. The communication to promote the Ten Miles is very elaborated. Both Golazo Sports and the city of Antwerp use social media (e.g., Facebook, Instagram and paid advertising). In addition, the city of Antwerp experimented with four influencers from target groups and uses the traditional channels (i.e., posters and billboards). However, the communication of the Corrida is rather limited. A flyer is developed by DCLA, which is distributed to the local sports administration and last year's participants. The city of Leuven promotes the event by means of their website, posters and in the monthly city magazine. Social media is not used (and also not necessary, as the organisers put a cap on the number of participants). However, in the 2019 edition, a three-hour live coverage of the event was provided, in cooperation with a local broadcaster (which was unique in Flanders).

DCLA does not organise any side events to promote the Corrida, mainly because the event is carried out by volunteers of the athletics club (no professionals) and thus they do not possess the right (human) resources (see also Table 4.4 in Chapter 4). On the contrary, different side events are linked to the Ten Miles. These side events are mainly carried out by organisations associated with different parts of the event. The fee for participation is rather low for the Corrida and rather high for the Ten Miles. The city of Leuven encourages local clubs to organise events in order to keep prices low (as well as to create local involvement). In that way, multiple (target) groups are able to participate. For the higher participation fee for the Ten Miles, participants get more in return, such as several free drinking stations and music bands along the course, and a medal at the finish.

The Corrida is only financially supported by three parties (among which is the local administration). This is mainly due to the fact that DCLA is not or cannot be professionally involved in strategically looking for additional funds (see earlier). The Ten Miles, however, receives financial support from several large organisations. Sponsors can buy packages that allow them to capture certain parts of the event (e.g., the title sponsor of the event receives an extensive preparatory trajectory with activation and targeting on the field which is not offered to lower-contributing sponsors; another company claims the title sponsorship of the business village and its visibility is limited to that part of the event).

Both events have attractive event courses. On the one hand, DCLA offers a cosy course with three different distances within the Leuven ring road along the different sights of the city. On the other hand, Golazo Sports is able to offer a course that allows participants to both run through different tunnels which are only accessible by car and along the beautiful city centre.

Events impact

The impact of the two Flemish running events is discussed by taking a look at mobility issues (for a negative example of physical impact, see Chapter 4) and revenues for local business (for a positive example of economic impact, see Chapter 4) as these were both experienced as very important impacts by the event organisers (Alexandris et al., 2021). After all, and as indicated in Chapter 4, the majority of running events do not have the resources to deliver the full spectrum of event impacts.

First, both running events had to impose a cap on participant numbers for comfort and safety of participants in the past as there are restrictions related to public gatherings and safety. Streets closure is unavoidable during running events, which impacts local businesses and residents. The start and finish locations of the Corrida are still easily accessible as Leuven is not an immensely large city and participants can easily park their car outside the ring road and walk towards the event or take public transport to the city (centre). As regards the Ten Miles, the accessibility of the start and finish locations is somewhat more cumbersome as participants need to reach the city's left bank.

Most people arrive on the city's right bank and there is no bridge between the two banks (only one tunnel for cyclists, one tunnel for walkers, one ferry and four tram lines).

Second, both events realise revenues for local businesses. The Corrida is organised on the last Sunday of the year, often between Christmas and New Year's Eve. In that way, many people can do their last Christmas shopping. The Ten Miles is traditionally organised on the last Sunday of April, which is a shopping Sunday in the city as well. Not only participants spend some money in local businesses, but the numerous spectators as well.

Take home messages

Based on the foregoing, some take home messages can be provided to local sports administrations, event organisers and event stakeholders in general. These are set up, based on recommendations provided by Helsen et al. (2020).

a Local sports administration
  - Generate a well-developed and well-thought sports event policy (e.g., different running events throughout the whole year) with a targeted marketing campaign (e.g., to guide participants from one event to another event). Ideally, this sports event policy is integrated in a broader sports, exercise and health policy that focuses on a healthy and active lifestyle. Additionally, the public sector has an important role in designing and building attractive and exercise-friendly environments throughout the city (which can be used during running events; see also Chapter 2).

b Event organisers
  - As also indicated in Chapter 3, the event concept is crucial. Therefore, organisers of running events should generate a clear event goal/event identity and make choices to achieve that goal or to linger to that identity (e.g., by using targeted side events).

c Event stakeholders in general
  - Determine which impacts the event organiser or local sports administration want to achieve. Usually, event stakeholders are short in time and resources to realise event impacts (see also Chapter 4). Therefore, event

stakeholders should appoint a person or organisation in advance that is responsible for keeping track of reaching these impacts (both before as after the event).
- As also indicated in Chapter 2, there is a need for collaboration between providers from different profit sectors. Therefore, event stakeholders should strive for coopetition (cooperation + competition) instead of competition.
- Measuring is knowing: (long-term) data is important to evaluate policy and initiatives, as well as make substantiated decisions for future policy, management and marketing.

Notes

1 Companies can pay to have a booth in the business village near the start and finish lines. These booths can be used by the company employees as a base during the event. The employees are encouraged to participate in the event as means of teambuilding or to adopt an active lifestyle. However, many businesses see opportunities to network in the business village. In the 2022 edition, more individuals participated via their company (group inscriptions) compared to private inscriptions.
2 Abbreviation for *Daring Club Leuven Atletiek*. The club was founded in 1942 and nowadays has about 800 affiliated members.

References

Alexandris, K., Barkoukis, V., Karagiorgos, T., Ntovoli, A., de Brito, M., Middelkamp, E., Mitas, O., van Liere, L., Ahonen, A., Girginov, V., Di Tommaso, V., Moliterni, S., Ruggeri, A., Helsen, K., Scheerder, J., Kreivyte, R., Mejeryte-Narkeviciene, K., Valantine, I., Hover, P., & van Eldert, P. (2021). *Promoting health enhancing physical activity and social welfare through outdoor running events. Case studies report* (RUN for HEALTH Project Report 5). Thessaloniki: Aristotle University of Thessaloniki.

Helsen, K., Scheerder, J., Girginov, V., & Ahonen, A. (2020). *Policy recommendations to promote health-enhancing physical activity and social welfare in the EU. Results based on the European RUN for HEALTH project* (Sport Policy & Management Studies 75). Leuven: KU Leuven/Policy in Sports & Physical Activity Research Group. https://gbiomed.kuleuven.be/english/research/50000737/groups/policy-in-sports-physical-activity-research-group/spm-studies/copy_of_bms75-spm.pdf (accessed 12 July 2022).

Helsen, K. & Scheerder, J. (2020a). *AG Antwerp 10 Miles & Marathon 2019. Results based on the European RUN for HEALTH project* (Sport Policy & Management Infographics 73). Leuven: KU Leuven/Policy in Sports & Physical Activity Research Group. https://gbiomed.kuleuven.be/english/research/50000737/groups/policy-in-sports-physical-activity-research-group/spm-studies/copy_of_spm-infographic-73-finaal-20201125-twitterlink-1.pdf (accessed 12 July 2022).

Helsen, K., & Scheerder, J. (2020b). *Eindejaarscorrida Leuven 2019. Results based on the European RUN for HEALTH project* (Sport Policy & Management Infographics 74). Leuven: KU Leuven/Policy in Sports & Physical Activity Research Group. https://gbiomed.kuleuven.be/english/research/50000737/groups/policy-in-sports-physical-activity-research-group/spm-studies/copy_of_spm-infographic-74-finaal-20201125-twitterlink-1.pdf (accessed 12 July 2022).

3 Marketing running events

Kostas Alexandris, Paul Hover, and Linda Ooms

This chapter deals with the marketing aspects of running events. Event marketing is a structured way of designing strategies in order to achieve the event objectives, which can be related to economic impacts, tourism, physical, socio-cultural, psychological and political impacts (see also Chapter 4 for the different kinds of impacts). The core of the marketing concept is a focus on the consumer, in this case primarily the event participant, although spectators can be a target group, too. Successful marketing flows from a complete understanding of the consumer (Bowdin et al., 2006). In this line, marketing of a running event has three main aims: (1) promoting the event's visions and goals; (2) engaging participants and relevant stakeholders and (3) communicating the positive events' impacts of the event, so that these can be used to continue to motivate the event's audience to participate again. It is important to realise that the event's visions and goals, target audience, desired impacts and the marketing of the event are closely interrelated where the first three influence marketing actions and vice versa. For marketing to be of added value, the traditional four P's (Product, Price, Place & time and Promotion) of marketing have to be considered (Beech & Chadwick, 2007; Kok & Gruijters, 2013). Furthermore, it's critical that these elements of the marketing mix are coordinated. It is not the goal of this chapter to cover in detail all the elements of the marketing mix. Rather, based on our experience, it suggests some topics which are deemed important in marketing running events. Also, practical suggestions to enhance the marketing (strategy) of running events are provided. Finally, two cases studies of running events, i.e., the Marathon Amersfoort (in Amersfoort, The Netherlands) and the Athens Marathon: the authentic (in Athens, Greece; henceforth Athens Authentic Marathon), are included to illustrate the key marketing characteristics discussed.

DOI: 10.4324/9781003301691-3

The product of running events

For a running event to be successful, the event concept is crucial. Elements like the vision and goals, theme, audience and venue need to be compatible for the event concept to be successful. Running events belong to the sport service industry because they exist to serve the needs of participants and spectators, and their delivery requires the provision of a range of information, security, medical, insurance and other services. As such, they can be seen as a 'product' with four unique characteristics of sport services, as discussed by Funk, Alexandris and McDonald (2022, in press):

- *Intangibility*: The product of a running event is largely intangible; it cannot be touched, being perceived by senses, and it does not have clear physical evidence. This creates challenges in defining, communicating and promoting it.
- *Heterogeneity*: The delivery of running events cannot be standardised; it is difficult to guarantee consistency in service quality, since there are several external factors that influence it; many of them are not under the control of the organisers. Examples are the weather, the runners' attitudes and performance, the running conditions, accidents which might happen, but also the recent COVID-19 measures that were put in place and influenced the organisation and delivery of running events dramatically. Furthermore, there is a high degree of subjectivity in evaluating running events' services. Runners' perceptions regarding services are largely subjective, since they are based more on personal needs and expectations and less on specific attributes, as it is in the case of industrial products. The question of what a quality running event is needs to be answered with reference to the profile and expectations of runners which might change over time (see also Chapter 2 and Section 'promotion' of running events in this chapter).
- *Perishability*: The time element has a great influence on running events. The date of the event is fixed months in advance; if the number of registrations is low, the event will still have run, with possible financial losses (see also Section 'place and time' of running events in this chapter).
- *Inseparability*: Running events are produced and consumed simultaneously. A city marathon takes place (is produced) in a city and is consumed at the same time and the same place by the runners. In this sense, most work considering the running event, including marketing actions, is done on the day of the event. This creates

risky situations, since any problems during the operation of the event, such as accidents and deficiencies in the delivery, are visible to runners, spectators and even media consumers.

It is important to take these characteristics of running events as a product into account when developing the running concept. Furthermore, when developing the running concept, it can be helpful to analyse the product of running events according to Zeithaml and Bitner's (2003) three service level analysis, including the core product, the tangible product and the augmented product:

- The *core product* can be defined based on runners' expected benefits and solutions provided during the event. In order to define it, participants needs have to be identified. Research has shown that for leisure running events enjoyment and entertainment are among the main runners' needs (Theodorakis et al., 2019). However, expected benefits relate to the profile of the runners (see also Chapter 2) and the focus of the event. For the most 'serious' runners, competition and achievement can be the main motives (see also Section 'promotion' of running events). The core product of some running events is then developed based on the actual race and its technical and competitive characteristics.
- The *tangible product* includes all the 'visible' aspects of running events; elements that runners and spectators can 'feel', and 'touch'. Examples can be employees, volunteers, the runners, the running route, the facilities, sport equipment, the supportive stations, the communication material, the website, etc. The tangible part of the event helps marketers to create the visual image of the event and build the brand. The 'visible' elements are part of the communication strategy (see also Section 'promotion' of running events).
- The *augmented product* includes all supportive services provided by organisers in order to enrich the value of the event and improve the experience of runners and spectators. Enhancing the core product of running events has a strategic value, since research has shown that the supportive services can help the event to build its image and differentiate itself from the competition (Alexandris et al., 2018). Also, it can help to attract people to the running event that would normally not attend a running event, such as inactive people.

Finally, the typology of running events described in Table 1.1 in Chapter 1, which includes twelve different dimensions of running events, can be helpful in understanding the visions and goals of the event, how these can be promoted and impact on people and places. This typology is, therefore, useful in developing the running product and positioning it in the running event market.

Marketing implications

The following are some key suggestions for developing the running product or 'running concept', especially the core and tangible products:

Concentrate on a type of impact and target audience

In order to develop a successful running concept and optimise the impact of a running event, it is important to make choices regarding the type of impact that is aimed for and the target audience. A running event may, for example, contribute to stimulating healthy behaviours, mental and social well-being, and/or economic or environmental impact (see also Chapter 4). The main objective of the Marathon of Amersfoort is, for example, to stimulate a positive attitude towards health, sport participation and physical activity among local residents and focuses therefore on recreational runners with a broad age range. The choice for the type of impact and target audience depends on the concept and wishes of stakeholders, including the target audience and local government. It is also recommended to decide on this topic when it is clear on which groups other running events in the country aim at and which impact they primarily strive for. In doing so, one can rationally position the running event in the running event market.

Co-create the running event concept

To enhance support for and participation in the event, it is important to co-create the running event concept, which was done both in the Marathon of Amersfoort and in the Athens Authentic Marathon. The target audience can be seen as more than just running event consumers. They are co-producers (Crawford, 2004) because an important part of the event is created by them. This can be achieved by actively involving the target audience and relevant stakeholders in the development of the concept. This is also a good strategy in order to develop and deliver a modern event concept. The list of an event stakeholders is rather long but critical among them can be considered the organising committee, the runners, but also, sports clubs, local authorities, local communities, and (potential) sponsors. It has to be noted that the majority of running events are public and their main role is the creation of public value. Local authorities have a main role in promoting public value and social benefits. Subsequently, they expect that events should create opportunities for collective benefits for the community in order to support them (for a more detailed discussion on running events and public value, see Chapters 2 and 4). In the Marathon of Amersfoort, the local government was one of the stakeholders, while the Athens Authentic Marathon is supported by the local government and other governmental tourism and sport agencies

Co-creation will not only help to enhance support and participation in the event, but will also result in the target audience and stakeholders embracing it as their own. Sports clubs in the neighbourhood could, for instance, help in the organisation or provide facilities (e.g., dressing rooms) or training programmes to prepare for the event. Local organisations could, for example, sponsor the event, offer help in its promotion or provide healthy food and drinks to participants and visitors. The local government should be involved to enhance and support the public value of the running event, but also to obtain the necessary licenses (e.g., for temporary road closures). In addition, the local government could facilitate the event in other ways such as by providing access to (sport) facilities. Support of the local community for the event is important, especially if the event is large and when it takes place in public space, which is frequently the case with recreational running events. Locals can be seen as hosts, as well as potential participants. People are, for example, more likely to participate in sport events that are close to their homes (Ooms et al., 2015). Ideally, there should be strong support among the local population. Local support also contributes to resilience in coping with negative effects such as possible temporary road closures and noise disturbance.

The following practical suggestions relate to the augmented product:

Organise auxiliary activities

Organising auxiliary activities or side events is a way of running event leveraging. Leveraging refers to the way the event and its resources are exploited in order to produce desired effects (Chalip, 2006; Hover & Slender, 2018; Taks et al., 2015). In this regard, the impact of one running event can be seen as a drop of ink falling in a bucket of water, for a moment the colour is visible and creates a beautiful surface, but a few seconds later it is not visible anymore. More targeted activities around the event should ensure more drops eventually giving colour to the water (Hover et al., 2016). Nonetheless, successful leveraging is absent in a significant number of events, partly because of inadequate knowledge, and sometimes unwillingness to invest time and resources in activities that go beyond the running event itself. Typically, the main event manifests itself as a 'greedy institution', absorbing all the time and money and leaving little energy for thinking about and acting on activities that extend well beyond the closure of the event (Hover et al., 2016). Therefore, it should not be the running event organiser that organises the auxiliary activities, but other (partner) organisations, in close coordination with the event organiser.

The use of side events, such as a sports promotion campaign, a school project, a music or cultural festival, is of added value in terms of leverage. As mentioned before, side events can be organised, for example, for people who would normally not be attracted to the running event, such as inactive people. Making links with other domains, such as culture and the arts may therefore bear fruit. Also, the creation of places where participants, visitors and other stakeholders can meet, such as fan zones, VIP lounges and catering squares can enhance the attractiveness of and experience with an event, and simultaneously enhance social connectedness among people. Side events and other derivative activities can take place before, during and after the event. To promote running and a healthy lifestyle, the Marathon of Amersfoort, for example, organises various side events for local residents (e.g., free running training sessions and a movie evening) throughout the year. The same applies for the Athens Authentic Marathon, where several side events are organised giving the event the image of a running festival, in which an active lifestyle is promoted.

Support the core product with appropriate services from the destination in which the event takes place

Another way to enhance the value of and experience with a running event and to make it attractive is to offer services from the event's destination. On a small scale, this can be done by creating an attractive offer around the event of relevant local products (e.g., local foods and sport services), which can simultaneously enhance the economic impact of an event. On a larger scale, comprehensive packages can be offered. These could include a visit to the event combined with other activities such as visiting side events, restaurants, cafes and museums, shopping, and tourist tours. Furthermore, multi-day visits can be stimulated during which participants, spectators and other stakeholders spend the night in an overnight accommodation. The longer people (participants and spectators of the event) stay in a certain area, the more they will spend on local products and services. However, this should be actively deployed by offering suitable accommodation options. It is, therefore, important to collaborate with local hotels, bed and breakfasts or other accommodations were people can stay. In order to offer suitable packages for participants and other visitors, it is important to have knowledge about who these people are. This will be further discussed in the section about the promotion of running events.

The place and time of running events

The selection of the place of the running event is an important decision, since research has shown that the destination influences many runners' and their associated people's decision on which events to participate (Theodorakis, Kaplanidou, Alexandris, Papadimitriou, 2019). Research also suggests that the characteristics of a destination in which an event takes place can contribute to the development of an event's image. This is particularly the case when a destination holds historical, mythological and cultural connotations, such as with the Olympus Marathon (Greece), but also with the Athens Authentic Marathon (Greece) and the Marathon of Amersfoort (The Netherlands), in which the running routes pass highlights of the city or larger area (Alexandris et al., 2019). Media coverage of the running event can incite persons who followed the event via the media to visit the host city after the event. This is called the showcase effect (Fredline et al., 2004; Hiller 1989). The selection of the right place is therefore dependent on the vision and the goals of an event. Examples are the promotion of a city/region, the development of a tourism destination and the promotion of a nature area. The selection of the place is also dependent on the desired impact of an event. Running an event in nature, for example, can create positive mental experiences, while running an event in a city with many people can promote social experiences. Locating the event in a city centre or an area with many good local services, could contribute to the economic impact of an event. The physical and transport accessibility aspect is also an important factor that needs to be considered.

In addition to the place of the event, the timing of the event is of importance. The timing of the event can be, for example, related to the goals or vision of the event, the relation of the event with certain (historical) moments such as with the Athens Authentic Marathon, the season (e.g., weather conditions and holidays), the available infrastructure (e.g., availability of public transport, options to close roads and availability of volunteers) and desired impacts (e.g., when the aim is to increase tourism and you may want to organise the event during holidays). Not only the timing during the year, but also timing on a day can be relevant. It is, for example, best to start a marathon early in the morning, so that it is not to warm and people have enough time to finish the marathon during the day. Night running races are also organised, as in the case of the Alexander the Great night half-marathon in Thessaloniki, Greece.

Using the typology of running events, as discussed previously, can also be helpful in making decisions about the 'place' and 'time' concepts.

Marketing implications

Choose an event location that is easily accessible by public or active transportation

When choosing a location for the running event (and side events), the assumption should be that people do not necessarily have to use the car to reach it. It is, therefore, important that the location of the event (and side events) is near to a bus or train station and can be reached on foot or by bicycle. The Marathon of Amersfoort is a good example, in which the start and finish of the marathon take place on the Eem Square in the city centre, a location easy to reach and 800 metres from the central train station. These ways of transport should also be attractive to participants and spectators. This can be done by providing participants and spectators with information on safe walking and cycling routes to the event, creating sufficient bicycle parking facilities, informing public transport companies about the expected crowds, and looking for possibilities for discounts on public transport or combination tickets (European Healthy Stadia Network, 2014).

Choose an event location that offers possibilities to add additional local services

As mentioned in the previous section, additional local services added to the event can enhance the augmented product. Therefore, when this is required a suitable event location that offers these possibilities should be chosen. A good example is the Women's Trail in Zell am See, Kaprun (Austria; https://womens-trail.com/). This is a three day trail running event specifically aimed at women, which offers different packages, including local goods, overnight stays and workshops from local (sport) providers.

The promotion of running events

The promotion of running events includes all formal and informal communication activities using both traditional and digital communication media, undertaken to attract the target audience and other people to the running event and also to develop positive attitudes towards repeated attendance. To create an appropriate promotional strategy, it is important to know the characteristics, needs and wishes of the target audience. In this regard, market segmentation is often used. Also, branding of the event and using appropriate communication channels are important. These will be discussed in the next sections.

Market segmentation

Market segmentation is defined as "the process of dividing a market, in this case the market of (potential) runners, into distinct subsets of consumers with common needs or characteristics and selecting one or more segments to target with a distinct marketing mix" (Schiffman & Kanuk, 2004, p. 33). Segmenting runners into homogeneous groups can help event organisers and marketers to identify their unique needs, deliver services according to their needs and position events in a way to promote their competitive advantages. In this sense, market segmentation does not only help in developing an appropriate promotional strategy, but can also help in developing a running product that fits the needs and wishes of the target audience. However, it is good to realise that the running market and thus runners' profiles may change over time (see also Chapter 2). So this means that the running product and accompanying promotional strategy may need adjustments over time depending on the running market and the target audience.

There are several segmentation criteria, with the most common being: demographics (age, gender, family type), socio-cultural (e.g., social class, race and ethnicity), geographic (e.g., urban and rural), behavioural (e.g., frequency of service use and quantity of product buying), and psychographic (e.g., attitudes, benefits, motivation and personality) variables (Funk et al., 2022, in press). While demographic, socio-cultural and geographic criteria can be easily applied based on runners' information provided through standard registration process, the behavioural and psychographic variables are more difficult to be applied, since they require primary behavioural research. In this regard, both qualitative and quantitative research can be used. However, when the focus is on non-runners, such as inactive people, more in-depth primary research is needed, because the target audience is not yet 'visible' for the organiser of the event. Demographics can be used to define who the runners or non-runners are, while psychographic variables can give information on runners' or non-runners' decision-making process for (non-)participating in running events and evaluate their post event and future behaviour. A good example is a study conducted in the USA (Rohm et al., 2006) where runners were classified in four groups by using a combination of demographic, behavioural and psychographic data:

- *Healthy Joggers*, who are mainly motivated by fitness and health-related motives, they have some experience from running and have an average age of 40–50 years old.
- *Social Competitors*, who are motivated by physical, mental health, competition and social-related motives and have the highest percentage of runners more than 50 years old.
- *Actualised Athletes*, who are mainly, motivated by self-esteem and fitness related motives and they are the less experienced runners.
- *Devotees*, who are addicted to running. They run the most miles per week, participate in several marathons per year and they have an average age of 25–50 years old.

A second example is presented in the study by Borgers et al. (2015) among Belgian/Flemish runners. Based on motives and attitudes towards running, the authors proposed the following five segments: (a) the individual runner (40.9%), (b) the social-competitive runner (25.9%), (c) the social-community runner (17.6%), (d) the health and fitness runner (9.0%) and (e) the performance runner (6.7%).

It is clear that each of the above groups has different motives, expectations and requirements. This means that the running concept and the branding and communication strategy for each group can be different.

Another example is the Run4Health project in which the profile of runners of twelve specific events in Greece, Holland, Belgium, Italy and Lithuania (see Table 1.2 in Chapter 1 for the characteristics of these events) was examined based on socio-demographic and psychographic variables. With regard to the latter, two important psychographic variables were included: runner's motives for participation and involvement levels.

Examining runners' motives for participation is an important element of profiling runners, since satisfaction of motives and expectations will bring repeated behaviour/attendance. Results from the Run4Health project indicate that fitness, social, competition and achievement were the four main dimensions of motives, as reported by the runners (Alexandris, Karagiorgos, Ntovoli, et al., 2019).

Further, the involvement construct is one of the psychographic variables that can be used for profiling runners. Getz and McConnell

(2014) reported that highly involved runners participate in more events, consider the characteristics of the running destination for tourism purposes, are willing to travel to international destinations, stay longer and tend to travel with their partners or family members. All these are positive behaviours for maximising the tourism and economic impacts of running events. Involved runners also consider the image of the event and use several criteria for choosing it. As Getz and Andersson (2010) elucidate these criteria relate to both the event itself and its attributes but also to the attributes of the destination, in which the event takes place. Alexandris et al. (2019) also suggested that for the most involved runners, the core aspects of the event, which are related to the technical attributes, the route and the quality of the actual race are the most important criteria to choose and evaluate the event, while for the less involved athletes the peripheral (supportive) aspects of the event are valued more. This again shows that segmentation of runners is not only helpful in promoting a running event, but also complements other P's of marketing (product, place and time).

The three-dimensional involvement model including the dimensions attraction, centrality and self-expression (Kyle et al., 2006) was used in the Run4Health project to profile runners. Data were collected in 2018 and 2019 from running events in Belgium, Greece, Lithuania and Netherlands. Attraction refers to the degree to which running is considered as an enjoyable and fun activity, centrality refers to the degree to which running has an important role in a runner's everyday life and self-expression measures runner's identification with the activity itself. Attraction was the highest scored dimension in all the event runners meaning that runners perceive running as a fun, enjoyable and excited activity. Scores in the centrality dimension were the lowest ones but still medium to high in actual values, which means that running has an important role in runners' everyday life. Finally, scores in the self-expression dimensions were also medium to high, which shows that runners identify themselves with the activity and see running as a way to express themselves and develop their running identity.

In term of the age, in all the events the average age of runners was over 35 years, with the Greek event having the highest one (43 years old). Males were the majority in all the events as well. However, in the events in Belgium and Netherlands the percentage of women runners was relatively high (>.40%). It is significant that the majority of runners in all the events were university graduates. This is in accordance with the findings in Chapter 2 where it is stated that recreational running mainly attracts people with a rather higher social status. Urban events are the most popular events. However, around 20% of runners participate also in events that take place in nature. It seems that events create positive feelings for participants in all the countries, which supports previous research that running is associated with positive psychological outcomes and improved well-being (Malchrowicz-Mo'sko & Poczta, 2018; Theodorakis et al., 2019). Finally, the findings of this project also showed that running events do act as a motivator for increasing the training of runners before the event and promoting an active lifestyle after it, which is also confirmed by other studies (Ooms et al., 2013; Schoemaker et al., 2019).

Marketing implications

Invest enough time and resources in getting to know the target audience

From the above, it is clear that event organisers should invest in developing detailed knowledge about their target audience. Knowledge about target audiences can be obtained by primary research. As mentioned before, both qualitative (e.g., interviews) and quantitative (e.g., questionnaires) research methods can be used to obtain information about the target audience. It is important that enough time is reserved for performing this research before advancing to development of a running concept and a promotional strategy. A research institute could perform the research, but when limited resources are available also students or volunteers could be used to perform the work. In essence, investing in knowledge about target audiences contributes to the successful development of a running concept (product), promotion and delivery of the running event.

Branding of running events

A brand is defined as "a name, terms, sign, symbol, or design, or a combination of them, intended to identify the goods and services of one seller or group of sellers and differentiate them from those of competition" (AMA, https://www.ama.org/, n.d.).

Branding running events is necessary in order to create distinct profiles and differentiate them from the competition. The typology of running events, as mentioned before, can be utilised before making branding decisions. Events with strong brands can build participants' loyalty and enhance repeated participation, through the development of effective communication and trust with the runners (Alexandris et al., 2016). Two elements are important for the development of a strong brand profile: the positive brand associations and the building of the event's brand personality traits.

Keller (1993) defined brand associations as "informational nodes linked to the brand node in memory and contain the meaning of the brand for the consumers" (p. 3). Positive brand associations can be developed when runners link events with positive benefits, attributes and attitudes. The benefits relate to satisfying their expectations for taking part in an event (e.g., "participation in the event helped me to socialise, to test myself, etc"). The attributes relate to runners' cognitive evaluation about the quality of the event. These evaluations are made when the actual experience (after participating in the event) is compared with the expected one (before participating in the event) and the outcome is positive. Finally, attitudes can also have an affective element related to runners' positive feelings, which are developed when participating in the event. Strong positive brand associations in all three elements above can contribute towards building the brand equity of the event.

Azoulay and Kapferer (2003) defined brand personality as "the set of human personality traits that are both applicable and relevant for brands" (p. 151). This definition proposes that, as individuals have specific personality profiles determined by their traits (see also Section 'Market segmentation'), products and services might also have distinct personality profiles, based on traits attributed to them.

Alexandris (2016) proposed that running events can have their distinctive image and personality, which is determined by both the attributes of the event itself (i.e., the running event product) but also by the characteristics of the destination in which they take place (i.e., the place and time of the running event, e.g., Mountain Olympus). This is one of the unique characteristics of running events, since the attributes and the image of the destination can contribute to the development of the event associations and their personality, especially in cases where the destination holds historical (e.g., the Athens Authentic Marathon), mythological (the Olympus Marathon) and cultural (On the Tracks of the Bear: Metsovo Race) connotations, or having its own strong brand (e.g., the London Marathon).

Events with distinct personality profiles can be associated with several positive behavioural outcomes, such as repeated/participation through the development of brand preference, brand equity, psychological attachment and involvement with the event and its activities (Aaker, 1997; Hosany et al., 2006; Keller, 2003).

The most used brand personality framework, which was also applied to the setting of running marathons, is Aakers' (1997) five-brand personality trait model. It proposes that the following facets should be measured in order to define the personality of a brand:

1 *Sincerity*: a tendency of a brand to be perceived as down to earth, honest, wholesome and cheerful.
2 *Sophistication*: the degree to which a brand is perceived as upper class and charming.
3 *Excitement*: a tendency of a brand to be perceived as daring, spirited, imaginative and up-to-date.
4 *Competence*: the degree to which a brand is perceived as reliable, intelligent and successful.
5 *Ruggedness*: a tendency of a brand to be perceived as outdoorsy and masculine.

From the above dimensions, Alexandris (1996) proposed that the excitement, sincerity and competence are the most applicable dimensions in the context of running events, while the ruggedness depends on the type of the event.

An excited event is the one being perceived as enjoyable, cool and fun, but also unique and contemporary. It has to be noted that participation in running events is still a 'trendy' activity today. Furthermore, Alexandris et al. (2020) reported that runners expect to develop positive feelings when running an event. Running events should also have a healthy image, as they are linked with healthy behaviours and an active lifestyle (Scheerder et al., 2020). Finally, the use of technology can also give the image of a contemporary event.

A sincere event is linked with family oriented and "small town related perceptions" (Aaker, 1997). In more recreational-oriented events like city marathons, runners view participation as an opportunity to run with family members and promote healthy family lifestyles. There are events which are positioned based on the social aspect (e.g., Run Together, in Greece). The "small town related perceptions" are developed when local communities support events, which as previously noted, is an important strategy for successful branding of an event (see also the case study LIfeSouth Run Weekend in Chapter 4). Finally, Aaker (1997) linked sincerity with the perception of a product being original and authentic. In the case of running events, the theme of the event is part of the branding process. Historical, cultural, environmental and even educational themes can create the feeling of an event being authentic and original.

The competence dimension relates to the degree to which an event is perceived as reliable, intelligent and successful. This dimension reflects the strength of the brand of running events. Those events which have high awareness levels and strong brand equity are considered as 'leaders' in the running market and are perceived as successful by runners and spectators. High event image is usually associated with reliability and trust towards the event organisers.

Finally, the personality-ruggedness dimension is developed in the case of events which have a more competitive nature. There are events which are physically and technically demanding and they are positioned as such (e.g., Marathon des Sables, 2016; The Jungle Ultra Marathon Beyond the Ultimate: Nothing Tougher). It is a strategic decision to be made by the organisers should they wish to develop their event image as a 'tough' one and position it like this in the competition.

Marketing implications

Develop a distinctive and appropriate running event concept

As mentioned above, the running event concept is the basis of a successful running event. Event organisers should focus on the development of a distinctive and appropriate event concept. For instance, the concept of a running event can be built around the theme of 'innovation', but also around 'festivity' and 'inclusion'. The involvement of local communities can help towards branding an event, in the concept of cocreation and communication. The goals of the event should fit well with the local or regional policy agenda to enhance public value. This increases the chance of local support, cooperation, synergy and positive effects. Promoting the strengths of the local population or host region can also help towards developing a strong event concept. Examples are running events which contribute to a charity, a colour run or an event with a concept that fits the desired profile of the host region. An illustration of the first is the case study of the LifeSouth Race Weekend in Florida (https://runsignup.com/Race/FL/Gainesville/LifeSouthRace Weekend, see Chapter 4), and of the second is the Marathon Eindhoven in The Netherlands, which aims to become the most innovative marathon worldwide. This ambition fits the host region as the Eindhoven region promotes itself worldwide as a smart city with the key concepts of technology, knowledge and innovation (and design) (Eindhoven municipality, 2019, https://www.marathoneindhoven.org/).

Communication strategy

On deciding the communication and positioning strategy, it is important for organisers to first define on the running product or concept, the brand personality, and, of course, the target audiences that they want to attract. The selection of appropriate communication messages and media comes next. While runners' motives and expectations may vary depending on the type of the event, it can be argued that most of the running events have a 'healthy' image, linked with healthy behaviours and associative personality traits. It can therefore be argued that associating running events with physical and psychological health-related behaviours can be an appealing communication strategy for a large number of running participants. As previously discussed, people participate in running events not only for physical activity or for sport performances, but also consciously or unconsciously for mental well-being and socio-psychological benefits. The experience of strong emotions, adrenaline, pleasure, relaxation and an opportunity to build social relationships are all examples of reasons for adults to participate in a running event. For children and adolescents, motivations are predominantly related to fun and enjoyment (Malchrowicz-Mo´sko et al., 2020; Malchrowicz-Mo´sko & Poczta, 2018). There are, however, cases of events which target the more 'serious' leisure runners, for whom, as discussed previously, competition, personal challenge and achievement-related motives drive their event participation. The communication strategy is therefore different in these types of events, since images, messages and solutions should be appealing to the most serious runners.

Furthermore, it has to be noted that there are several running events which focus on philanthropic activities and donations. In such events, runners are motivated by philanthropic values and subsequently the communication strategy should appeal to philanthropy and social values. Examples are the Susan G. Komen Race for the Cure (https://www.komen.org/) the Parkinson's Half Marathon and 5K (https://parkinsonshalfmarathon.com/), the Race for Life series evens (https://raceforlife.cancerresearchuk.org/about-our-events), and the aforementioned The LifeSouth Race Weekend. In addition, 'Green events', 'green marketing' and 'green places/destinations' are concepts that can be incorporated within the marketing and communication strategy of events as well, and they can also be used as themes in branding the events. Runners are usually environmentally sensitive individuals and are more likely to be attracted by environmental friendly events (Davies et al., 2019).

It is not the objective to discuss all different communication tools that can be used by event organisers. However, it should be noted that at present social media as a promotional, communication and monitor tool is a prerequisite in all running events. This is due to the community nature of runners which makes targeted communication (e.g., through blogs and social media channels) more effective than mass communication, considering also the costs and the limited communication budgets. Social media has become an important tool for increasing consumer engagement, which brings involvement and the development of psychological attachment. Studies among sport fans have provided evidence for the important role of digital marketing in creating environments that promote fan engagement with the team, players and associative activities (Trivedi et al., 2021). Event organisers should develop strategies to engage runners in the actual event, if involvement is to be built and repeated behaviour to be developed. Runners' reaction to organisers' posts on event related activities is a simple indicator of the effectiveness of the social media communication. Two examples from the Run4Health Project related to the use of social media as a promotion and monitoring tool are presenting below:

Social media monitoring was used for the Marathon of Amersfoort and Vestingloop Den Bosch in The Netherlands to establish the social impact analysis. With the help of an online media monitoring tool, OBI4WAN, the posts on Facebook, Twitter and blogs by social media users were analysed with the view to address the question "what responses were generated by the event posts and individual users' posts".

The Marathon of Amersfoort holds 6,095 followers on Facebook and 1,659 followers on Twitter. The monitoring of these social media took place from the 29th of April 2019 – 15th of July 2019. In total, 250 messages were posted. First of all, it became clear that there was a distinction on social media between professional runners and leisure runners. As an outcome, it can be seen that many posts from leisure runners were related to participants looking for their running photos. There were some complaints about not enough pictures being taken and shared and about the duration of the organisation to post them online. One popular health/training related topic discussed was the progression by training for the event. Social media users have posted something about training together, working on breathing, movement and the start of the run.

In a second example, The BrandLoyalty Vestingloop in The Netherlands, the analysis showed that it holds 9,080 followers on Facebook and 1,411 followers on Twitter. The monitoring of these social media took place from the 29th of April 2019 – 15th of July 2019. In total, 1,203 Facebook and 258 Twitter interactions were examined. The first thing that became clear was the high level of engagement on the content of the posts of the Vestingloop on Facebook, which, as discussed before, is a highly desirable outcome of social media communication and one of the indicators of evaluating the effectiveness of the communication strategy. There were many people tagging others to challenge them to sign up for the run. There were some health-related topics discussed, such as water tap points along the track, motivation from people and personal records.

In summary, the marketing and communication strategy of running events should be based on a clear event concept, and a distinct event personality profile. Developing runners' involvement with the event is one of the main strategies to attract and retain runners and spectators. Social media and digital marketing are the most effective tools today for building runners' and spectators' involvement and loyalty with an event.

Marketing implications

Promote the running event in a way that is appealing to the target audience

From previous and this section, it is shown that people participate in running events for different reasons. Different types of running events will attract different types of audiences. Therefore, it is important to use proper promotional messages and channels to reach the right target audience. As mentioned before, messages relating to, for example, the health benefits or social outcomes of running events, can attract people who want to become fit or participate in the event to experience sport with others. While social media are for most runners a suitable promotional channel, for the older runners or youngest ones, other promotional channels may be necessary. These aspects should be considered when marketing the event to a specific target audience. For the Marathon of Amersfoort, for example, also adverts were placed in local newspapers and flyers and leaflets were distributed at local sport shops, running clubs and schools.

Conclusions

Marketing running events has to take a professional approach, since the market is mature and competitive. The runners and spectators are getting more and more experienced, and their needs and expectations are changing, following the changes in the external consumer and marketing environment. We have discussed important aspects of marketing, which all have to be considered, because they are interrelated. Moreover, this chapter shows that time and resources for marketing need to be reserved and marketing needs to be carefully planned. A detailed profile of the runners and spectators is, for example, necessary, based on socio-cultural, behavioural and psychographic variables in order for event organisers to be able to meet and facilitate their needs. At the same time, we proposed that decisions related to the branding of an event and the development of a distinct personality profile are important ones for effective positioning and differentiation within competition. Decisions related to branding an event and developing a distinct personality profile relate to event policy issues, the vision and goals of the stakeholders and the types of impacts that the event aims to achieve. These issues will be discussed in details in the following chapter. On closing this chapter, it has to be noted that social media and technology can play an important role in promoting and branding running events, following the general trend in the sport market, with the increased use of technology during and after the COVID-19 period. In this chapter, we did not discuss marketing aspects of digital running events, which were rapidly grown during the COVID-19 pandemic period.

References

Aaker, J.L. (1997). Dimensions of brand personality. *Journal of Marketing Research, 34*(3): 347–356.
Alexandris, K. (2016). Testing the role of sport event personality on the development of event involvement and loyalty: The case of mountain running races. *International Journal of Event and Festival Management, 7*(1): 1–20.
Alexandris, K., Karagiorgos, T., Ntovoli, A., Helsen, K., Scheerder, J., Hover, P., Eldert, P. van, Girginov, V., Brito, M. de, Middelkamp, E., & Mitas, O. (2019). *Promoting health enhancing physical activity and social welfare through outdoor running events. Run for Health*. Literature review.
Alexandris, K. Theodorakis, N., Kaplanidou, K., Papadimitriou D., (2018). Event quality and loyalty among runners with different running involvement levels: The Case of "The Alexander the Great" international marathon. *International Journal of Event and Festival Management, 8*(3): 292–307.
AMA, Branding. https://www.ama.org/topics/branding/
Azoulay, A., & Kapferer, J.N. (2003). Do brand personality scales really measure brand personality? *The Journal of Brand Management, 11*(2): 143–155.
Beech, J., & Chadwick, S. (2007). *The marketing of sport*. Harlow: Pearson Education Limited.
Bowdin, G., Allen, J., O'Toole, W., Harris, R., & McDonnel, I. (2006). *Events management*. Oxford: Elsevier Ltd.
Borgers, J., Vos, S., & Scheerder, J. (2015). Belgium (Flanders). Trends and governance in running. In: J. Scheerder, K. Breedveld & J. Borgers (Eds.). *Running across Europe. The rise and size of one of the largest sport markets* (pp. 28–58). Basingstoke: Palgrave Macmillan.

Chalip, L. (2006). Towards social leverage of sport events. *Journal of Sport & Tourism*, *11*(2): 109–127.
Crawford, G. (2004). *Consuming sport: Fans, sport and culture*. London: Taylor & Francis.
Eindhoven municipality (2019). Nota digitalisering van de stad [Memorandum on the digitization of the city].
European Healthy Stadia Network (2014). *Active travel guidance for sports stadia*. Liverpool: European Healthy Stadia Network.
Fredline, L., Raybould, M., Jago, L., & Deery, M. (2004). Triple bottom line event evaluation: Progress toward a technique to assist in planning and managing events in a sustainable manner.
Funk, D., Alexandris, K., & McDonald, H. (2022, in press). *Sport consumer behavior: Marketing strategies* (2nd Ed.). London: Routledge.
Getz, D., & Andersson, T. (2010). The event-tourist career trajectory: A study of high-involvement amateur distance runners. *Scandinavian Journal of Tourism and Hospitality*, *19*(4): 468–491.
Getz, D., & McConnell, A. (2014). Comparing trail runners and mountain bikers: Motivation, involvement, portfolios, and event-tourist careers. *Journal of Convention & Event Tourism*, *15*(1): 69–100.
Hiller, H. (1989). Impact and image: The convergence of urban factors in preparing for the 1988 Calgary Winter Olympics. In: G.J. Syme, B.J. Shaw, D.M. Fenton, & W.S. Mueller (Eds.). *The planning and evaluation of hallmark events* (pp. 119–131). Avebury: Aldershot.
Hosany, S., Ekinci, Y., & Uysal, M. (2006). Destination image and destination personality: An application of branding theories to tourism places. *Journal of Business Research*, *59*(5): 638–642.
Hover, P., Dijk, B., Breedveld, K., Eekeren, F. van, & Slender, H. (2016). *Creating social impact with sport events*. Utrecht: Mulier Institute.
Hover, P., & Slender, H. (2018). Sociale impact van sportevenementen: State of research [Social impact of sport events: State of research]. Den Haag: Nederlandse Sportraad.
Kok, R., & Gruijters, H. (2013). *Sportmarketing, derde editie*. Amsterdam: Pearson Benelux bv.
Keller, K.L. (1993). Conceptualizing, measuring, and managing customer-based brand equity. *Journal of Marketing*, *57*(1): 1–22.
Keller, K.L. (2003), *Strategic brand management: Building, measuring and managing brand equity* (2nd Ed.). Englewood Cliffs, NJ: Prentice-Hall.
Malchrowicz-Mo´sko, E., Castañeda-Babarro, A., & Guereño, P.L. (2020). On the way to the marathon-motivation for participating in mass running events among children and adolescents: Results of the Poznan half marathon pilot study. *International Journal of Environmental Research and Public Health*, *17*(4): 5098.
Malchrowicz-Mo´sko, E., & Poczta, J. (2018). Running as a form of therapy socio-psychological functions of mass running events for men and women. *International Journal of Environmental Research and Public Health*, *15*(10): 2262.

Ooms, L., Veenhof, C., & de Bakker, D.H. (2013). Effectiveness of start to run, a 6-week training program for novice runners, on increasing health-enhancing physical activity: A controlled study. *BMC Public Health, 13*: 697.

Ooms, L., Veenhof, C., Schipper-van Veldhoven, N., & de Bakker, D.H. (2015). Sporting programs for inactive population groups: Factors influencing implementation in the organized sports setting. *BMC Sports Science, Medicine and Rehabilitation, 7*: 12.

Rohm, A.J., Milne, G.R., & McDonald, M.A. (2006), Proven top-rate qualitative analysis and mixed methods research. *Sport Marketing Quarterly, 15*(1): 29–39.

Schiffman, L.C., & Kanuk, L.L. (2004). *Consumer behavior* (8th Ed.). NJ: Prentice Hall.

Schoemaker, J., van Genderen, S., & de Boer, W.I.J. (2019). Increased physical activity in preparation for a women-only mass participation sport event: A framework for estimating the health impact. *International Journal of Environmental Research and Public Health, 17*(1): 98.

Taks, M., Chalip, L., & Green, B.C. (2015). Impacts and strategic outcomes from non-mega sport events for local communities. *European Sport Management Quarterly, 15*(1); 1–6.

Theodorakis, N., Kaplanidou, K., Alexandris, K., & Papadimitriou, D. (2019). From sport event quality to quality of life: The role of satisfaction and purchase happiness. *Journal of Convention & Event Tourism, 20*(3): 241–260.

Zeithaml, V.A., & Bitner, M.J. (2003). *Services marketing: Integrating customer focus across the firm* (3rd Ed.). New Delhi: Tata McGraw-Hill.

Case study 3.1 Marathon Amersfoort, The Netherlands

Paul Hover and Linda Ooms

Running in public spaces has long ceased to be seen as an activity for weirdos, as was the case in the mid-1960s (Knight, 2018). Conversely, there are millions of people who run, without being in a hurry (Stokvis & Van Hilvoorde, 2008). The popularity of the participation in running has increased spectacularly in The Netherlands, as well as in other European counties (Hover et al., 2020; Scheerder & Breedveld, 2015). In 2020, 13% of the adult Dutch population ran at least once a week (in 2001, this was 4%). Accelerators of the increasing popularity of running are the growing number of recreational running events (and the variety in distances), the broadening of time limits (which makes events accessible to a greater group of people) and the combination of running with music and entertainment (resulting in a less intimidating character, opening the doors to a wider audience, Allison, 2010; Ridinger et al., 2012).

Over the past decade, the supply of running events has grown and competition between organisers has intensified (Baker et al., 2018). More than 1,200 small and large running events were included in the national running event calendar of the Dutch Athletics Federation in 2019, offering 5,200 event distances. One of these running events is the Marathon Amersfoort.

Product

The Marathon Amersfoort has been organised annually since 2012 and it is the largest running event in the province of Utrecht. In essence, the marathon is a service, principally for participants and visitors, which explains its mainly intangible social impacts. Because of Corona virus measures the event did not take place in 2020. The Marathon Amersfoort is owned by the Amersfoort Marathon Foundation, which has a board and an implementation committee responsible for organising the event. The distances for adults range from 5K up to the marathon, and the distances for children are of 1.1K and 2.2K. The idea is that by offering a broad range of distances, the event provides running opportunities for several target groups. Elite athletes rarely participate in the event and prize money is currently not offered. The costs for participation in 2022 vary from 14 euros (5K) to 45 euros (marathon). Pupils from schools in the local area can participate for free. Since 2018, the organisation serves walkers as a 21.1K walk has been added to the programme as well.

The event budget in 2021 amounted to 200,000 euros, of which 75,000 euro (37%) was subsidy from the local government, sponsors invested 32,500 euro (16%) and 92,500 euro (46%) was generated from registration fees. The organisation and design of the central Eem Square (stands, tents, sound, etc.) and traffic measures are among the largest cost items.

Place and time

Measured by number of residents, Amersfoort is the 16th largest municipality in The Netherlands. The city stands out with its medieval core with canals and ramparts. Since 2012, the finish of the marathon has taken place on the Eem Square in the city centre, a location easy to reach and 800 metres from the central train station.

The Amersfoort Marathon features a course that has proven to be a success among both participants and visitors. The route of the 21K and marathon runs along the river Eem, through Highland-West and via the Kattenbroek architecture district, across the canals of the old town. The last kilometres of all distances lie in the medieval setting in the city centre. The Amersfoort Marathon is organised in June. The 2021 event was an exception because as a result of national Corona virus measures the 2020 edition was moved to October 2021.

Type of impact

The primary objective of the organisation of the Amersfoort Marathon is to acquaint as many local residents as possible with the health effects of running, especially the local youth. In doing so, the marathon aims to contribute to the objective of the local government to stimulate physical activity and sport participation among residents. So, the prime type of the desired impact relates to nurturing positive attitudes towards health, sports participation and physical activity.

Furthermore, with the organisation of 25 performances of live bands, clowns, small orchestra, big bands and DJs along the course, the event successfully creates a festival effect (Weed et al., 2012). This type of impact refers to the attempt to create liminality, or an atmosphere, which transcends sport, where participants and visitors are in a state in which the structure and order of normal life dissolve and a momentary experience of a social bond between participants and visitors arises.

As to sustainability, the event organiser has been trying to create an impact too. Participants and visitors are encouraged to use public transport or a bicycle. The use of plastic drinking cups is abolished (biodegradable cups are used) and people are requested to bring their own drinking bottles instead of buying new ones.

Target audience

The Amersfoort Marathon is predominantly a recreational sport event with a focus on servicing inhabitants of the region. Habitually 5,000 runners participate in the event. Most of the participants reside in the city of Amersfoort (55%) and surrounding municipalities (15%). About 30% lives in other parts of The Netherlands or abroad. Notable is the diversity of nationalities among foreign participants. For example, in 2019 runners from 43 different nationalities participated. This is influenced by the relative scarce supply of city marathons in Europe in June. Additionally, 15,000 people visit the Marathon Amersfoort every year.

The Marathon Amersfoort Tracx App has been made available to participants and visitors. This app is technically linked to the EventApp platform of MYLAPS, a company which offers timing equipment and services (tracx.events/en). The app connects participants in 320 sporting events in four types of sport worldwide. In addition, visitors have the possibility to follow the progress of participants on the course. The app can increase participant and visitor experience positively.

Co-creation

As regards the organisation of the Marathon Amersfoort and auxiliary activities, the board and the implementation committee of the Amersfoort Marathon Foundation join forces with numerous local and regional partners. Sponsors, suppliers and partners include the local government, Meander Medical Centre, Run2Day Amersfoort (running shop), Run033.nl (platform for local runners), De Lieve Vrouw (theatre and cafe), B Slim Amersfoort (lifestyle programme for local youth), SKA (childcare), SRO (management of municipal real estate) and Sportivate (promotion of youth sports participation). Equally, the 5,000 participants and 15,000 visitors can also be seen as co-creators of the event because their role transcends the role of the consumer: participants and visitors are indispensable groups of people who contribute to the creation the event. Moreover, participants and visitors are co-creators of the running event experience too as an experience can be seen as a personal, memorable event with an emotional meaning (pleasure, adrenaline, relaxation), which comes about through an interaction with others (Wood, 2009). Lastly, the organisation of the Marathon Amersfoort works together with 'Dutch Marathons', a partnership between six Dutch marathons. This cooperation is largely centred around promotional activities.

Auxiliary activities

The activities of the organisation of the Amersfoort Marathon are not solely aimed at the organisation of the Marathon Amersfoort. During the year, numerous activities are organised, including free running training sessions, free ParkRuns (small-scale running activities in local parks), a movie evening, presentations about running and health, various fun runs and running clinics for kids. The purpose of the auxiliary activities is to promote running and a healthy lifestyle among local residents year-round. These activities are also aimed at facilitating the meeting of like-minded people. As such, auxiliary activities both strengthen and promote the marathon.

Promotion and communication

Several means of promotion and communication are put into practice, including traditional and digital promotion. Since 2018, the event has a website which provides comprehensive information for all stakeholders (www.marathonamersfoort.nl). The Facebook page has almost 6,500 likes from 5,900 friends and the Twitter account of the Marathon Amersfoort has 1,700 followers as of 2021. The Amersfoort Marathon has its own YouTube channel, with 26 self-produced videos (https://www.youtube.com/channel/UC0WAdJqtKbDXOsQj3-3mQ1g). Every two weeks, an article is published in a local newspaper which reaches 70,000 households. In the weeks leading up to the event, local outdoor advertising is organised. Furthermore, starting nine months in the run up to the event, an e-mail newsletter is sent every four weeks to 18,000 recipients (from one month before the marathon, the e-mail newsletter appears every two weeks). The organiser also advertises in popular running magazines and press releases are sent to both regional and national (sports) media. Leaflets and posters are distributed at relevant locations, including sport shops, running clubs and schools.

References

Allison, D. (2010). The unstoppable 21st-century marathon boom. *Marathon & Beyond*, *14*(5): 80–92.

Baker, B.J., Jordan, J.S., & Funk, D.C. (2018). Run again another day: The role of consumer characteristics and satisfaction in repeat consumption of a sport-related experience product. *Journal of Sport Management*, *32*: 38–52.

Hover, P., Eldert, P. van, & Oprins, I. (2020). *Hardlopen: grenzen aan groei: deelname aan hardlopen en hardloopevenementen [Running: Limits to Growth: Participation in Running and Running Events]*. Utrecht: Mulier Instituut.

Knight, P. (2018). *Shoe dog. A memoir by the creator of NIKE*. Amsterdam: Van Ditmar.

Ridinger, L.L., Funk, D.C., Jordan, J.S., & Kaplanidou, K. (2012). Marathons for the masses: Exploring the role of negotiation-efficacy and involvement on running commitment. *Journal of Leisure Research*, *44*(2): 155–178.

Scheerder, J., & Breedveld, K. (2015). *Running across Europe: The rise and size of one of the largest sport markets*. Houndmills, Basingstoke, Hampshire: Palgrave Macmillan.

Stokvis, R., & Hilvoorde, I. van (2008). *Fitter, harder & mooier: de onweerstaanbare opkomst van de fitnesscultuur [Fitter, harder &*

more beautiful: The irresistible rise of fitness culture]. Amsterdam: Uitgeverij De Arbeiderspers.

Theodorakis, N., Kaplanidou, K., Alexandris, K., Papadimitriou, D. (2019). From sport event quality to quality of life: The role of satisfaction and purchase happiness. *Journal of Convention & Event Tourism, 20* (3): 241–260.

Weed, M., Coren, E., Fiore, J., Wellard, I., Mansfield, L., Chatziefstathiou, D., & Dowse, S. (2012). Developing a physical activity legacy from the London 2012 Olympic and Paralympic Games: A policy-led systematic review. *Perspectives in Public Health, 132*(2): 75–80. DOI: 10.1177/1757913911435758.

Wood, E.H. (2009). Evaluating event marketing: Experience or outcome? *Journal of Promotion Management, 15*: 1–2, 247–268. DOI: 10.1080/10496490902892580.

Case study 3.2 Athens Marathon: The authentic

Thomas Karagiorgos, Apostolia Ntovoli, Panagiota Balaska and Kostas Alexandris

Running in Greece

The growth of running in Greece started around 2006. The Hellenic Association of Amateur Athletics (SEGAS; http://www.segas.gr) followed a strategy for promoting running all over the country. As a result, the number of outdoor running races grew from around 60 and 15,000 registered runners in 2006, to more than 936 races and 250,000 registrations in 2019. SEGAS' seven main running events were placed under the umbrella of 'Running Greece' races, which take place all over Greece throughout the year. One of these events is the Athens Marathon: the Authentic.

Product

The Athens Marathon: the Authentic is the largest running event in Greece and one of the largest running events internationally. It is organised by SEGAS. Besides the marathon, there is a 5 km and 10 km run. The event's growth during the last 15 years has been impressive. The number of runners increased from 5.250 in 2016 to 50.000 (850% increase) in 2019, which was the year before the COVID-19 lockdown. This growth has happened despite the years of economic crisis in Greece. The growth of the marathon can also be seen through other indicators. In 2019, the budget of the marathon was around 2 million euro (up from 300.000 euro in 2006, 666% increase). The sponsors' investments and economic activity (fees, supporting teams/runners, communication actions, activation, etc.) amounted to more than two million euro (Asimakopoulos 2016, 2018).

The product is enhanced during the years by relying on the experience and knowledge of the executives who worked for the 2004 Athens Olympic Games and on a team of professionals who worked full-time for the organisation of the event throughout the year. Furthermore, there have been investments in the upgrade of event services (see also auxiliary activities) and by changing it from a one day event to a four day festival with the inclusion of associative shorter running events for recreational runners, building in this way the augmented product of the event. Finally, investments were made in training volunteers who help in all the stages of the event operation (Asimakopoulos 2016, 2018).

Place and time

The 42,195m route starts at the Marathon Start Venue in the town of Marathonas. Runners follow the route that was mapped for the 1896 Olympic Games and it is supposed to be close to the route that Pheidippides followed bearing the news of victory (https://marathon.athensauthentic.com/en/The-Race). Pheidippides was a long-distance runner or courier in Ancient Greece. His accomplishment is an inspiration for the modern sporting event of marathon race.

Type of impact

It is estimated that the direct economic impact of the event on the city of Athens is more than 15 million euro (Alexandris et al., 2021). This economic impact comes from international runners and from those who are not residents of the city of Athens (more than 8,000 runners). The event has a strong focus on fundraising for social responsibility actions. More than 800,000 euro is collected and used for social purposes. Finally, the event has also an environmental programme, so that plastic bottles, garbage, clothes, etc., are collected and recycled, thus, promoting sustainability values at the same time. More than 3,000 volunteers participated, which in a structured volunteered training programme before the event is one of its strengths. It is important to emphasise that SEGAS has as a strategic goal to promote running as an everyday leisure activity, and not just one-time event participation during a year. Considering all the above characteristics, it is clear that the event and its auxiliary activities have a strong sport, social, economic, tourism and health impact on the city and its residents.

Participants/target audience

The socio-demographic characteristics of runners show their dynamic profile, in terms of both age and education (Alexandris et al., 2021). As shown in Figure 3.1, the vast majority of runners in all races are highly educated; graduates who constitute 76% of participants in the 5 km, 81% in the 10 km and 78% in the 42 km (Figure 3.1). Furthermore, the average age in all the races is just above 40 years (41.2 in the 5 km, 41.6 in the 10 km, and 43.4 in the 42 km, Figure 3.2). Finally, runners are almost balanced in terms of gender in the 5 km distance (51.4% males and 48.6% females), while males dominate in the 10 km and 42 km races (67.1%, and 81.5%, respectively, Figure 3.3).

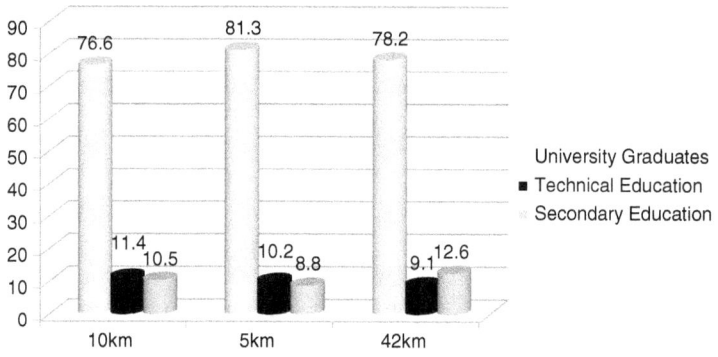

Figure 3.1 Educational level of runners by race.

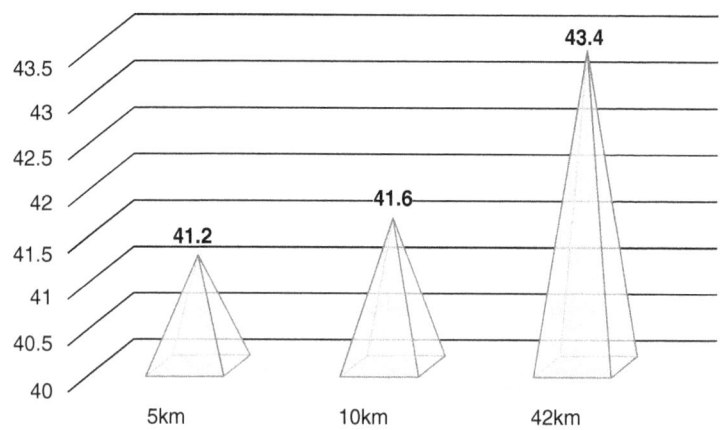

Figure 3.2 Average age of runners by race.

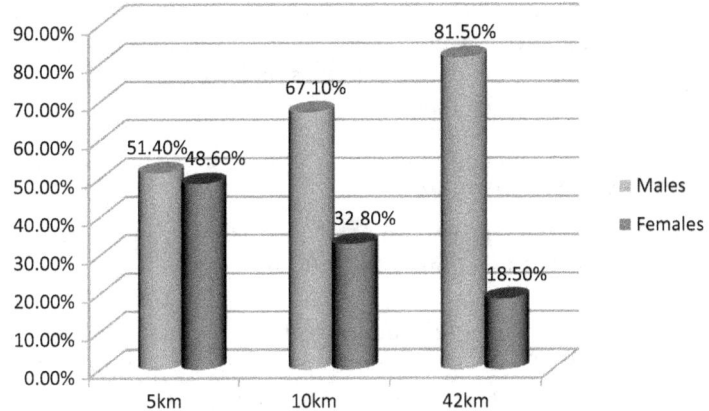

Figure 3.3 Gender of runners by race.

Co-creation and collaboration

For the event, there is cooperation with public bodies, private organisations and non-profit associations in order to maximise the impact of the event (Asimakopoulos 2016, 2018). Examples of these bodies include Local Authorities of Athens and Marathon, the Region of Attica, the Greek Tourism Organisation, EKAB, The Greek Police, OASA, etc. As discussed in this chapter, these partnerships are necessary in order for the event to be co-created and co-produced by the relevant stakeholders. Furthermore, local associations and communities are involved within the event organisation to build positive attitudes towards the event. Moreover, there is cooperation with 16 non-governmental organisations in order to reinforce social and environmental values, volunteerism, charitable causes and fundraising. The main goal of SEGAS was the event to be self-financed through strategic cooperation with private firms and sponsors. Some indicative sponsors include OPAP, AEGEAN, Adidas, ERT, ERGON, Stoiximan, Piraeus Bank, AVRA, Coca-Cola, Renault, Dole and Metropolitan Hospital.

Auxiliary activities

Using the analytical marketing strategy aspects discussed in this chapter, SEGAS' growth marketing strategy was not only focused on improving the core product (see the product section) and enhancing the impact of the event (see the impact section), but also developing auxiliary activities, building a strong brand and good international image.

Promotion and communication

Several marketing, promotion and communication strategies were developed (Asimakopoulos 2016, 2018):

- Taking advantage of the international reputation of Greece, as a result of successfully hosting the 2004 Athens Olympic Games and at the same time using the legacy of the Games.
- Changing the name of the event to "Athens Marathon: The Authentic", which was an important rebranding and positioning strategy.
- Managing to differentiate the event from the other marathons in Greece and in the world. The 'Authentic' aspect is a clear differentiation element and a clear positioning strategy.
- Promoting the history of the event and moving the Opening Ceremony to the archeological place of the Marathon Tymbo; this helped built a unique event concept.
- Establishing the travel of the iconic 'Marathon Flame' to four continents (Europe, Asia, North America, and Africa) and to more than 30 countries. The Marathon Flame was created by the Athens Classic Marathon Organising Committee, SEGAS and the Municipality of Marathon at a special ceremony near the Tomb of the Athenians in 2007. It has been adopted by AIMS (The Association of International Marathons and the road running affiliate of WA) and of the Marathon Movement worldwide. (https://antarctic-logistics.com/2012/11/20/marathon-flame-travels-to-union-glacier/).
- Giving an international image to the event with the establishment of the International Symposium of Marathon, with the participation of more than 60 running event organisers from all over the world and with the awarding of the best international marathon runners. This symposium helps to further build the augmented product of the event and differentiating it from other running events.

- Succeeding in locating the headquarters of the World Association of Marathons to the Olympic Stadium in Athens, which was a strategic move in order to further build the event image.

References

Athens Marathon: the Authentic. https://marathon.athensauthentic.com/en/The-Race

Asimakopoulos, M. (2016). How we reached on the miracle of the Athens Authentic Marathon, Retrieved from http://www.businessnews.gr/article/47895/pos-ftasame-sto-thayma-toy-marathonioyathinas#.V7YI1rEyW1k.email (In Greek)

Asimakopoulos, M. (2018). Athens Marathon: The Authentic, in Alexnadris (Ed), *Sport Tourism Management*, Ed: Thessaloniki: Kiriakidis, (in Greek).

Alexandris, K. Barkoukis, V.; Karagiorgos, T., Ntovoli, A., de Brito, M.; Middelkamp, E., Mitas, O., van Liere, L., Ahonen, A.,; Girginov, V.; Di Tommaso, V.; Moliterni, S., Ruggeri, A., Helsen, K., Scheerder, J., Kreivyte, R., Mejeryte-Narkeviciene, K., Valantine, Ir., Hover, P., & van Eldert, P. (2021). *Promoting health enhancing physical activity and social welfare through outdoor running events. Quantitative results*, RUN for HEALTH Project Report, Vol. 2.

Marathon Flame Travels to Union Glacier. Retrieved from https://antarctic-logistics.com/2012/11/20/marathon-flame-travels-to-union-glacier/

4 Running events' impacts

Vassil Girginov

The typology of running events established in the introductory chapter suggests that they come in different forms and serve a multitude of purposes. Thus, unlike highly standardised and recurring mega sporting occurrences such as the Olympic Games and World Cup, most running events (save some high-profile marathons or mass runs) do not possess the resource mobilisation potential allowing them to deliver the full spectrum of social, economic, environmental and sporting impacts. Nonetheless, what unites these events with their mega counterparts is an underlying sequential logic on which they are based. It entails that because of their sequential character, that is, running events represent something beyond themselves, and the fact that they need to mobilise material and human resources, these occurrences produce both tangible and intangible impacts.

Impacts epitomise the essence of running events and form a critical part of the logical chain underpinning this book. The first link of the chain is policy (Chapter 2), which put broadly articulates the vision behind the event and answers the key question 'why do we need to do this event?' The answer to this question contains not only a vision but a promise as well. The promise, on its part, entails interactions or an exchange between the event owners and participants. In these interactions, event organisers undertake actions to meet certain social, logistical and environmental requirements and to deliver some benefits in exchange for the right to use public resources and to alter people's normal daily routines. Owing to their popularity, universal access, low costs, and perceived benefits, running events have been considered by governments and promoters as 'lifestyle medicine' (Filo & Coghan, 2016). This broader understanding of the main role of running events presents a challenge to the conceptualisation and measurement of their impacts. This is because it is based on a positivist logic and its belief in causality and human ability to predict and control the future. The

DOI: 10.4324/9781003301691-4

framing of various events' visions bears the hallmark of positivism in that they purport a positive causal relationship between running and the occurrence of certain benefits.

A further understanding of the policy of running events requires us to pose two critical questions. The first one is 'how do visions of running events impacts come about?' That is, who formulates those visions, what processes have been followed and how were decisions made? The second question is concerned with 'how promises of impact are delivered and at what cost?'. The remainder of this chapter will try to provide answers to these questions.

The second link in the impact chain is marketing (Chapter 3). It serves a three-fold purpose, including promoting the event's visions, engaging participants and stakeholders and communicating the positive events' impacts, so that these can be used to continue to motivate the event's publics to participate again.

The final link in the chain is the impact (the current chapter) in terms of how it is delivered. The delivery will be contingent on several factors, including political and marketing. This chapter will first review the state of current knowledge on events and running events impact in particular, before examining the critical questions posed above.

Running events impacts: taking stock of current knowledge

The best seller 'The Complete Book of Running' (Fixx, 1979) exhorts the positive benefits to individuals who practise it but makes no mention of social or economic impacts at all. It is astonishing how during the past 40 odd years, running has moved beyond personal gains and expanded to include broader social, economic and sporting impacts. Literature on events impacts and legacy has grown exponentially over the past 20 years, including the first dedicated conference (De Moragas et al., 2003), books (Grix, 2014; Neri, 2020; Zimbalist, 2015), systematic reviews (Koenigstorfer et al., 2019; Scheu et al., 2021; Teare & Taks, 2021; Thomson et al., 2018) and corporate reports (DCMS, 2011; IOC, 2017). Nonetheless, as Teare and Taks (2021) note, research on sport participation impacts from sport events has been sporadic and marked by a limited and inconsistent use of theoretical frameworks. The lack of common understanding about impact is understandable, given that it is a multi-dimensional concept, involves different routes by which it may occur across contexts and that impact changes over time.

Events impacts have been variously defined depending on the theoretical perspective taken, the needs of organisations and the field in

Table 4.1 Impact types of running events

Type of impact	Examples of manifestations	
	Positive	Negative
Economic	Increased expenditures	Price increases during event
Tourism/commercial	Increased awareness of the region as a tourism destination	Risk of damaging reputation in case of improper practices
Physical	Improvement of local infrastructure	Overcrowding
Sociocultural	Increase in participation in activity associated with event	Commercialisation of activities of a private nature
Psychological	Increased local pride	Visitor or host hostility
Political	Propagation of political values held by government	Ego trips of individuals

Source: Adapted from Ritchie (1984).

which they take place. Table 4.1 provides an early typology of events impact and Table 4.2 summarises selected definitions of sociocultural impact of events, some of which encompass the broader concept of quality of life while others focus on value systems, attitudes and behaviours. While these definitions help gain a general understanding of the nature of impacts, they are not particularly useful for research and practical purposes as they require proper operationalisation, validation, testing and codification.

Impact evaluation has also been codified in the form of online tools to allow event organisers to develop valuable insights. Examples of dedicated sport impact tools include the eventIMPACTS (https://www.eventimpacts.com/), which is a collaboration between Department for Culture, Media and Sport, Discover Northern Ireland, EventScotland, London & Partners, UK Sport and Welsh Government, and the Sports Events and Tourism Association tool (https://www.sportseta.org/resources/event-impact-calculator). Similar tools for other aspects of events' impact such as city image in the form of an Event Impact Calculator (EIC) (https://destinationsinternational.org/event-impact-calculator) for the European market have been jointly developed by Destinations International and European Cities Marketing.

Events research also produces impact, and according to Research Council UK (n.d.), it could take three main forms, including (i) instrumental (i.e., influencing the development of policy, practice or services,

Table 4.2 Definitions of sociocultural impacts

Source	Definition
Fredline, Jago & Deery (2003, p. 26)	'Any impacts that potentially have an impact on the quality of life for local residents' (sociocultural impact)
Mathieson & Wall in Fredline (2005, p. 264); Ohmann et al. (2006, p. 130)	'Social impacts of tourism refer to the changes in quality of life of residents of tourist destinations'
Hall in Balduck et al. (2011, p. 94)	'Manner in which events effect changes in the collective and individual value systems, behavior patterns, community structures, lifestyle and quality of life'
Olsen & Merwin in Ohmann et al. (2006, p. 130)	'Changes in the structure and functioning of patterned social ordering that occur in conjunction with an environmental, technological or social innovation or alteration'
Ritchie in Inoue & Havard (2014, p. 297)	'Social impact of a sport event is the enhanced level of local pride, a sense of community and enthusiasm for the community among residents of a host community'

shaping legislation and changing behaviour), (ii) conceptual (i.e., contributing to the understanding of policy issues and reframing debates) and (iii) capacity building through technical and personal skill development. Studies on running events have provided evidence about their capacity to deliver those three impacts (Du et al., 2020; Olberding & Olberding, 2014; Xing et al., 2020). The case study on running events in China below illustrates nicely the above three forms of impact.

As far as can be ascertained, the most systematic and comprehensive attempt to examine the impact and legacy of a single mega event has been the meta evaluation of the 2012 London Olympic & Paralympic Games commissioned by the UK government. The research tool used in this evaluation was the logic model (DCMS, 2011), which has also been employed in other studies both within and outside sport. The logic model seeks to establish the expected causal link between impact activities through to their outputs and impacts and uses a 'theory of change' and relevant evidence. The model's theory of change is essentially a hypothesis that if, for example, people participate in a running event this may lead to positive benefits for their well-being. The logic model could be summarised as made up of five elements, including context (i.e., political, social and economic rationale for organising the event), resources (i.e., material and non-material available), inputs (i.e., activities and resources provided), outputs (i.e., what was produced-number of participants) and outcomes/impacts (i.e., what has changed as a result – attitudes, behaviours).

A main challenge faced by impact evaluations is the comparison with the counterfactual use, that is, what would have happened in the absence of the running event? When considered, the counterfactual urges examining the extent to which a running event caused a particular effect in participants and places. This way, any purported impact is narrowed down to a measurable change in a pre-specified variable.

All running events, regardless of their scale, have an impact where typically the larger the scale of the event, the greater its impact. Events impacts fall in two broad categories, including tangible (i.e., building new facilities, road improvements and job creation) and intangible (i.e., enhancing community spirit, people's self-confidence and place image), and could be planned and unplanned. Owing to the difficulties in documenting intangible impacts, most events promoters tend to focus on the tangibles and use them for promotional and resource-generation purposes. Given the typical one-day duration of most running events, their tangible impacts have been relatively limited, although they have the potential to stimulate national and international tourism and business activities. A rare comparative study by Gratton et al. (2006) of ten major sport events in the UK reported that the World Half Marathon Championship held in Bristol (the only running event in the sample) had the highest daily economic impact of £583,942, which was well above the rest of the events. Without exception, all running events studies by the Run4Health project have much greater stated intangible impacts such as healthy lifestyle benefits, which directly correlate with their broader well-being objectives.

Recent studies, however, show that the interaction between social (i.e., intangible) and economic (i.e., tangible) impacts is under-researched. As Mair et al. (2021) note, "the reality is that these impacts co-exist and overlap, and may even trade off, from pre, during and post analysis" (p. 17). Mair et al.'s (2021) systematic review of social impacts of mega events identified eight impacts, including direct impact on residents volunteering, education and skills, social cohesion, civic pride and social capital, inclusion and diversity, sport participation, infrastructure and health, impacts on destination ecosystem, business and government networks, destination branding, disaster preparedness and accessibility. Some of these impacts have been examined in the context of running events as well. For example, Zhou, Kaplanidou and Wegner (2021) found that trust, reciprocity and networks are the three core components of social capital among running events participants, and Pfitzner and Koeningstorfer (2017) documented the positive impact of corporate running events on organisational climate and employees. The work of Wallstam et al. (2020) concerns specifically the evaluation of social impact for policy purposes. The authors identify a set of six indicators which policy makers need to consider in determining whether to host a running event, and thus, establish a link between visions of impacts and their delivery. These include community quality of life; community pride; social capital; sense of community; community capacity enhancement and facilities impact. The study by Xing et al. (2020) illustrates Mair et al.'s (2021) point about the overlap between tangible and intangible impacts. Xing et al. (2020) examined the link between health, social and consumption capital on Chinese runners' expenditures and found that all three variables had a significant impact on the total running-related expenditures per year.

There have been several specific attempts for conceptualising the impacts of running events. Olberding and Olberding (2014) proposed and tested a framework for capturing the social impact of small events which brings together place marketing and social welfare. Place marketing's indicators include enhancing city image and brand and increasing local pride. The social welfare is operationalised through building community in strengthening social networks and supporting social causes. Building on the earlier work of Brown et al. (2015), Graefe et al. (2019) have integrated social, ecological and economic approaches in developing a comprehensive method for evaluating the impact of small-scale running events on public land. While the results from both studies are inconclusive, they nonetheless have promoted the need for a holistic approach to running events impacts.

As established above, running events impacts are premised on a promise between at least two parties, where one party (i.e., the event promoter) offers certain benefits to another party (i.e., events participants) in exchange of some resources and a mandate for action. It follows that events impacts emerge because of the interactions stimulated in the exchange. There is a paucity of studies examining aspects of participants' engagement with running events from an organisational and participants' perspective. Temerak and Winklhofer (2021) explored the full spectrum of how participants interact with running events by breaking engagement down to emotional, cognitive, behavioural and social dimensions. They found that fully engaged participants engage across the four dimensions, and that the presence of other participants stimulates social engagement. A central concept in understanding events interactions is that of satisfaction, which is directly related to the nature of impacts. Du et al. (2020) examined the collective role of euphoric, fitness, competition, social and entertainment benefits on runners' satisfaction. The authors highlight the complementarity of these motivational antecedents and the fact that event organisers ought "to provide services and strategies designed to cultivate and strengthen a sense of achievement, fitness and enjoyment derived from running prior to event day" (p. 444).

Visions of impact

How do event visions come about? Who decides on what an event should look like and how its visions of impacts are to be achieved? These are critical questions, which help us understand the nature of running events' impacts and their meaning for individuals, organisations and communities. Even the lonely individual runner expects and experiences some impacts before, during and after the run, including feeling energised and a sense of accomplishment by conquering a new distance, improved fitness or simply burning extra calories.

Running event impacts represent social constructions some of which are planned but others emerge unexpectedly and are beyond the control of organisers. From a planned event point of view, visions of impact represent forms of intentional development where one agency sets out to develop the capacity of another or to change it. Therefore, how the intent of development is bound to the process of development, that is, the delivery of impacts becomes of critical importance. This is because this process is responsible for both framing the impact visions by establishing what counts as 'impact knowledge' and positioning actors in the field as well as determining their relationships. The presence of intent is crucial because we assume that the actions associated with it lead to certain effects. Impact visions serve as a theory of change based on the 'if–then' proposition. Impact visions also serve as active construction of reality because they identify groups and issues in society that are deemed either underdeveloped or unacceptable. For example, whether a running event aims at tackling poor health and fitness, obesity, anti-social behaviour or unfavourable city image, these aims represent forms of intended development. The running event discourse then turns the public gaze towards those groups and issues by exposing them publicly on record while at the same time subjecting to public scrutiny the promises made in this regard by event promoters.

Framing is critical for the social construction of impacts as it serves as a signifier and meaning constructor and provides collective action frames. Framing describes the work of event promoters, which denotes an active, processual phenomenon that implies agency and contention at the level of reality construction. Agency in framing entails the evolving work of event owners and promoters while contention involves the generation of competing frames (Benford & Snow, 2000). According to Snow and Benford (1988), framing involves three core tasks, including 'diagnostic framing' (i.e., problem identification and attribution – e.g., lack of mental health awareness), 'prognostic framing' (i.e., expected outcomes and impacts – e.g., improved social contacts) and 'motivational framing' (i.e., achieving agreement – e.g., generating support from participants). It addresses two core interrelated problems of 'consensus mobilisation' (i.e., agreeing on the need to stage the event) and 'action mobilisation' (i.e., fostering practical actions in the context of the event). Therefore, running events framing represents a deliberate and goal directed process. A running's diagnostic frame could be the lack of physical activity, its prognostic frame then suggests that running will improve your health, and the role of the motivational frame will be to convince you to take part. From a management point of view, each frame corresponds to certain management activities, including research and analysis (i.e., diagnostic), strategic and operational planning (i.e., prognostic) and marketing (i.e., motivational).

The discussion below builds on empirical analysis of 12 running events in five European countries (Belgium-3; Greece-2; Italy-3; Lithuania-2 and The Netherlands-2), including five marathons, six mass events and a trail. These events have been framed over a sustained period ranging from five years (e.g., Bosland Trail, Belgium, established in 2018) to nearly 40 years (e.g., Florence marathon, established in 1984). Running events' objectives and purported impacts are closely linked to their identity and are critical for success. All events in the sample claim a rather broad range of objectives, including promoting health, fitness, education, community spirit, supporting good causes and providing fun and entertainment, among others. Despite most events' well-defined competitive focus, they also cater for broader audiences and try to accommodate diverse groups of people, including children, families, competitive and recreational runners, and people with disabilities. Well-defined impacts are critical for the events' identity, communications, management, and sustainability. A tension between 'competing vs completing' ethos exists in almost all events studied. This tension is hugely indicative of the focus of the event and its objectives and has ramifications for the event offer and impacts.

Table 4.3 shows a comparison between selected running events' goals, public support and impacts. The findings suggest that promoting

Table 4.3 Relationship between selected running events' goals, public support and impacts

Country	Event/Year established	Goals	Public support	Impact
Belgium	Eindejaarscorrida Leuven 1997	Enhance personal satisfaction of club members	Strong local support	Sociocultural
	AG Antwerp 10 Miles & Marathon 1986	To get everyone moving	Strong local support	Social-economic
	BoslandTrail 2018	Promote ecology	Strong local support	Social-environmental
Greece	Alexander the Great Intern marathon 2006	Promote physical activity and health	Strong local & support from National Athletic Federation	Social-economic
	Athens marathon 2018	Promote physical activity and health	Strong local & support from National Athletic Federation	Social-economic
Italy	Chiavari 2014	Promote physical activity and the region	Strong local & support from National Athletic Federation	Social-economic
	Ravenna marathon 2011	Promote well-being, arts and culture	Strong local & support from National Athletic Federation and UNESCO	Social-economic
	Florence marathon 1984	Promote physical activity and the region	Some local & support from National Athletic Federation	Social-economic
Lithuania	Bristonas half-marathon 2016	Promote physical activity and the region	Strong local & support from National Athletic Federation	Social intangible
	Citadele Kaunas marathon 2010	Promote well-being and physical activity	Strong local & support from National Athletic Federation	Social intangible

| The Netherlands | Brandloyalty Vestingloop 2006 | Promote physical activity and the region | No/low local involvement | Social intangible |
| | Marathon Amersfoort 1986 | Promote physical activity and the region | Strong local support | Social-economic |

healthy lifestyle is the main desired impact of running events. However, upon closer examination of the declared goals of these events, it becomes obvious that healthy lifestyle means different things to different people. A second important observation from the table concerns the level of public support for running events. Without exception, all event organisers noted the declining support from public authorities although it was still present in most cases. Given that those events take place on public spaces, that is, they ought to be sanctioned by local authorities, as well as the fact that their declared goals fit very well with the authorities' mandate, the lack of public support is concerning.

Delivering running events impacts

Positive running event impacts are not inevitable and do not always result automatically from staging the event. There is so much that could go wrong – from bad weather to low turn up, to poor publicity and organisation, and all these negative factors had been encountered in the above 12 running events. Planned events' impacts are intentional and are premised on interactions between the event promoter and participants. Ziakas (2015, p. 692) expands this understanding to include potentially all stakeholders, arguing that "leveraging should be the responsibility of a non-event community entity or coalition that embraces all the sectors and stakeholder groups securing wide support from residents and deploying local resources". It follows that impacts can be delivered through various interactions before, during and after the event.

To further unpack the delivery of impacts, a running event is conceptualised as a resource with two key broad dimensions, including symbolic and material, which lends itself to leveraging by various parties. From an organisation's point of view, resources fall into five types, including moral (i.e., legitimacy, integrity, solidarity support,

108 *Vassil Girginov*

sympathetic support and celebrity), cultural (i.e., artefacts, conceptual tools and specialised knowledge), socio-organisational (i.e., infrastructures, social networks and organisations), human (i.e., labour, experience, skills, expertise and leadership) and material (i.e., monetary resources, property, office space, equipment and supplies) resources (Edwards & Gillham, 2013, pp. 3–4). Table 4.4 uses Edwards and Gillham's (2013) typology of organisational resources to illustrate them from a running event perspective, based on the sample of 12 events studied by this book.

A major challenge for most event resources is that they cannot be utilised in their original form but through a process of resource development, so they become more usable commodities. Sponsors' cash or in-kind support still needs to be put in use by a process of utilisation, including setting up structures, exchanges, monitoring and reporting mechanisms for which event organisers ought to have sufficient capacity. The concept of leveraging running events for impact is useful here. It brings to the analysis a high degree of rationality because it combines in one whole the strategic intent of an organisation to develop its own or the capacities of another agency (or that of a group of people), the professional skills, processes, resources and monitoring mechanisms required to do that as well as the specific timeframe within which this is to be achieved. It also promotes a traditional 'inside-out'

Table 4.4 Running events resources

Resource	Running event example
Moral (i.e., legitimacy, integrity, solidarity support, sympathetic support and celebrity)	Support from local authorities, national governing bodies, high-profile political figures; established in public calendar of events
Cultural (i.e., artefacts, conceptual tools and specialised knowledge)	Part of city/country heritage; high level of operational codification
Socio-organisational (i.e., infrastructures, social networks and organisations)	Links with other local running and cultural events
Human (i.e., labour, experience, skills, expertise and leadership)	Strong volunteers' and professional event companies' involvement; established organisational committees
Material (i.e., monetary resources, property, office space, equipment and supplies)	Commercial sponsorship, use of dedicated/historic routs

business logic concerned with the needs of the organisation, as illustrated by the case study of LifeSouth Race in the United States below. The logic model discussed in the previous section captures these elements over the life course of the event by moving systematically from context, resources, inputs, throughputs, outputs and impacts. It ought to be pointed out though that there could be substantial differences in the leveraging strategies of different stakeholders. This is a particularly important issue for running clubs and national governing bodies of athletics/running as their plans are usually developed on a four-year (Olympic) cycle basis. This means that if the event is not in their calendar, it will significantly limit the opportunities for its leveraging for sport development purposes.

There is a growing body of literature on sport events leveraging but running-specific studies are still a rarity. While the number of extant sport events leveraging frameworks is limited (Chalip, 2004; Fairley & Kelly, 2017; Misener, 2015), the array of events' leveraging aspects is almost indefinite. The common denominator of various leveraging models is the resource provided by the event, which is to be used as a 'hook' to maximise their impact. The event resource is multifaceted and may include the unique running subculture (Green, 2001), city image (Grix, 2012), hosting community (Peric et al., 2016), or its inspirational potential (Girginov, 2016), among others. These resources could be leveraged to deliver community (Taks et al., 2015), social (Ma & Kaplianidou, 2021), ecological (Dolles & Soderman, 2010), economic (Preuss, 2015), sporting (Girginov et al., 2017) or political (Schneider et al., 2020) impacts.

The delivery of running events' impacts is contingent on the events objectives, resource mobilisation potential, stakeholders' level of engagement and target publics. Ultimately, however, the impact is always in the eye of the beholder. This means that the value of the same running event will resonate differently in the different publics' mind. As established, running events are public occurrences, which project beyond themselves and their main role is the creation of public value. The notion of public value is of fundamental importance for understanding the impacts of events, but with some notable exceptions (Foley et al., 2015), it has been largely neglected in sport studies.

The concept of public value in the context of intangible Olympic legacy has been rehearsed previously at some length elsewhere (Girginov & Preuss, 2021). The current discussion focuses on four key points. First, the main thrust of the notion of public value concerns the critical role of public authorities for the functioning of society and an explicit concern with the 'collective', which resonates with the stated objectives of most running events. Mazzucato (2018) makes a convincing argument that there can be no value outside the public sphere. Her observation relates to the organisation of running events which are contingent on the political, logistical and financial support of public authorities. Thus, if public authorities do not see the collective benefits for the community, their support for the event may not be forthcoming. Second, Meynhardt (2009) proposes that value emerges "as a result of a relationship between a subject that is valuing an object and the valued object. Value does not exist independently outside of that relationship" (p. 198). He further elucidates that public value is perceived and not delivered and is always relative (Meynhardt, 2015).

In essence, the public value of a running event represents a relationship between a subject (i.e., participant and sport club) that is valuing an object and the valued object (i.e., the event). Third, it is critical to establish 'who is the public' which will be contingent on political, sociological or legal considerations. Running events have multiple publics, including participants, sport clubs, national governing bodies, volunteers, local authorities and sponsors, among others. Byers et al. (2019) echo this view and argue that the delivery of legacy of sporting events depends on stakeholders' interpretations and interactions. Finally, it is critical to understand why running events impacts get evaluated. Different publics will have different reasons to evaluate their relationship with an event, but the fundamental question asked by any stakeholder is "what makes the running event valuable for me?" When asked this way, the question shifts the focus from the general claims of purported events' benefits to the subjective perceptions and experiences of individuals, organisations and communities. As Meynhardt (2009) asserts, "value is bound to evolving relationships and ongoing processes of subjective evaluations and revaluations" (p. 199). Therefore, it would be reasonable to assume that subjects' evaluation of the impact of running events will evolve over time. None of the studied events had undertaken or commissioned an independent impact evaluation apart from selectively monitoring of social media exchanges.

Without exception, the 12 running events across the five countries investigated in this book, had multiple publics ranging from children, families, people with disabilities, recreational and competitive runners, athletic clubs, local authorities, sponsors, visitors and media (see Table 1.2). The overall impacts of the running events have been mainly sociocultural and intangible, and these were confined to the participants and local community, as evidenced by the low number of participants. The four established marathons (i.e., Alexander the Great,

AG Antwerp, Amersfoort Marathons and Ravena) were able to draw larger numbers, which automatically brings with it a greater number of supporting personnel, visitors and media attention. The relationship between the events' objectives, participants and impacts is a complex one as it entails reconciling the narrow interest of a local running club concerned mainly with meeting the needs of its 1,000 members (i.e., Daring Club Leuven Atletiek-Eindejaarscorrida Leuven) with the wider social agenda promoted by the city. Hence, the public value created by the event will look very differently for different stakeholders.

Further, only six (50%) of the running events had the support of the national governing body of athletics and only one event, the Alexander the Great Marathon in Greece, had leveraging for sports development as an explicit objective. Naturally, the small running event sample analysed here is not sufficient to draw definite conclusions about the value attached to these events by different stakeholders. Nonetheless, it is worth mentioning that most of these events have been framed as inclusive and appealing to wider publics. Even the traditional professional marathons would include auxiliary events such as 5k and family runs to attract more participants and to generate festival-like atmosphere.

A novel approach to leveraging of an established running brand for impact by improving participation from deprived communities has been proposed by Schneider and colleagues (2020, 2019). The authors studied the relationship between deprivation, distance and parkrun (a 5k free run) participation. The aim of the study was to provide policy and management recommendations for establishing the optimal location of new parkrun events. It was found that a careful space design would improve the average distance to the nearest parkrun event by 1.22 km, from 4.65 km to 3.43 km, and approximately 82% of the English population would live within 5 km of a parkrun event.

The two cases in this chapter richly illustrate at micro and macro levels the critical questions posed at the beginning, including how visions of impact come about and how promises of impact are delivered and at what cost. The LifeSouth Race Weekend in Gainesville is organised by a charity organisation which has nothing to do with sport but is concerned with blood donation. The triple social framing of the running event has allowed the organisers to align it successfully with the wider personal and social benefits produced by taking part in running. The diagnostic frame identified the irreplaceable importance of blood donation for the preservation of human life, the prognostic frame connected running to enhanced education, awareness, and a feelgood factor of doing something for the common good, and the motivational frame has convinced the business and civic community to take part. Thus, the visions of LifeSouth Race's impact have emerged through the leadership of the LifeSouth Community Foundation in consultations with local business and political elites. Despite being a local event, these findings echo the wider trend that mega sport events are projects of the political and business elites as they require the commitment of significant resources (Gold & Gold; 2016; Surborg et al., 2008).

In contrast, the case study on running events in China provides a macro perspective on the precursors to impact by focusing on national and local polices and governance changes responsible for preparing the conditions for maximising the impact of individual events. Visions of impact were shaped by the introduction of policies and were accompanied by relevant structural changes. The acquisition of running events by big media and IT companies has helped the promotion of running events in China, their structural legitimisation (through formal certification) as well as shaped their impacts locally and nationally.

The impact delivery has also been done with the collective efforts of local sporting organisations, educational organisations, local authorities and business agencies. The specific impacts generated by the two running events could be classed as tangible and intangible. Tangible impacts include fund-raising for the Foundation, business activities (including some part-time jobs creation) and tourism. The intangible impacts concern creating feelgood factor, enhancing city, university and sponsors' image as well as community cohesion. Despite the involvement of the Gainesville Sport Commission, there is no evidence for capacity building in local sport organisations, but it was present in China, promoted mainly by national and local public policy.

In conclusion, this chapter has established that running events' impacts are intrinsically linked (albeit not always easily discernible) to broader public well-being policies. Visions of impacts and their delivery are reflections of those policies and both model and mirror social lives. Running events' impacts are also shaped by local context and global political and economic environments but ultimately the public value they create is in the eye of the beholder.

References

Benford, R., & Snow, D. (2000). Framing processes and social movements: An overview and assessment. *Annual Review of Sociology, 26*: 611–639.

Brown, S., Getz, D., Pettersson, R., & Wallstam, M. (2015). Event evaluation: Definitions, concepts and a state of the art review. *International Journal of Event and Festival Management, 6*(2): 135–157. DOI: 10.1108/ijefm-03–2015-0014.

Byers, T., Hayday, E., & Pappous, A. (2019). A new conceptualization of mega sports event legacy delivery: Wicked problems and critical realist solution. *Sport Management Review, 23*(2). DOI: 10.1016/j.smr.2019.04.001.

Chalip, L. (2004). Beyond impact: A general model for sport event leverage. In: A. Darnel and B.W. Ritchie (Ed.). *Sport tourism: Interrelationships, impacts and issues, channel view publications* (pp. 226–252). Channel View Publications: Bristol.

DCMS (2011). Meta-evaluation of the impacts and legacy of the London 2012 Olympic Games and Paralympic games summary of reports 1 and 2: 'Scope, research questions and strategy' and 'Methods'. London: DCMS.

De Moragas, M., Kennett, C., & Puig, N. (Eds.). (2003). *The legacy of the Olympic Games 1984–2000*. Lausanne: IOC.

Dolles, H., & Söderman, S. (2010). Addressing ecology and sustainability in mega-sporting events: The 2006 football World Cup in Germany. *Journal of Management & Organization, 16*(4): 587–600.

Du, J., Kennedy, H., James, J., & Funk, D. (2020). Leveraging event participation benefits beyond the running course: Deciphering the motivational basis of event satisfaction. *Journal of Sport Management, 34*: 435–446.

Edwards, B., & Gillham, P. (2013). Resource mobilization theory. In: D.A. Snow, D. della Porta, B. Klandermans & D. McAdam (Eds.). *The Wiley-Blackwell Encyclopedia of social and political movements* (pp. 1–6). Oxford: Blackwell Publishing Ltd.

Fairley, S., & Kelly, D.M. (2017). Developing leveraging strategies for pre-games training for megaevents in non-host cities. *Marketing Intelligence and Planning, 35*(6): 740–755.

Filo, K., & Coghlan, A. (2016). Exploring the positive psychology domains of well-being activated through charity sport event experiences. *Event Management, 20*(2), 181–199.

Fixx, J.F. (1979). *The complete book of running*. Washington: Wahlström & Widstrand.

Foley, S., McGillivray, D., & McPherson, G. (2015). Culturing sports mega events: Leveraging public value. In: J.M. Bryson, B.C. Crosby & L. Bloomberg (Eds.). *Creating public value in practice* (pp. 331–347). Boca Raton: CRC Press/Taylor and Francis.

Girginov, V. (2016). Has the London 2012 Olympic Inspire programme inspired a generation? A realist view. *European Physical Education Review, 22*(4): 490–505.

Girginov, V., Peshin, N., & Belousov, L. (2017). Leveraging mega events for capacity building in voluntary sport organisations. *Voluntas: International Journal of Voluntary and Nonprofit Organizations, 28*(5): 2081–2102.

Girginov, V., & Preuss, H. (2021). Towards a conceptual definition of intangible Olympic legacy. *International Journal of Event and Festival Management, 13*(1): 1–17.

Gold, J., & Gold, M. (2016). *Olympic cities: City agendas, planning, and the world's games, 1896–2020*. Abingdon: Routledge.

Graefe, A., Mueller, T., Taff, D., & Wimpey, J. (2019). A comprehensive method for evaluating the impacts of race events on protected lands. *Society & Natural Resources An International Journal, 32*(10): 1155–1170.

Gratton, C., Shibli, S., & Coleman, R. (2006). The economic impact of major sports events: A review of ten events in the UK. *The Sociological Review*, 54(2_suppl): 41–58. DOI: 10.1111/j.1467-954X.2006.00652.x.

Green, C. (2001). Leveraging subculture and identity to promote sport events. *Sport Management Review*, 4(1): 1–19. DOI: 10.1016/S1441-3523(01)70067-8.

Grix, J. (2012). 'Image' leveraging and sports mega-events: Germany and the 2006 FIFA World Cup. *Journal of Sport and Tourism*, 17(4): 289–312. DOI: 10.1080/14775085.2012. 760934.

Grix, J. (Ed.). (2014). *Leveraging legacies from sport mega-events*. Basingstoke: Palgrave.

Inoue, Y., & Havard, C.T. (2014). Determinants and consequences of the perceived social impact of a sport event. *Journal of Sport Management*, 28: 295–310.

International Olympic Committee (IOC). (2017). *Legacy strategic approach: Moving forward*. Lausanne: IOC.

Koenigstorfer, J., Bocarro, J., Byers, T., Edwards, M., Jones, G., & Preuss, H. (2019). Mapping research on legacy of mega sporting events: Structural changes, consequences, and stakeholder evaluations in empirical studies. *Leisure Studies*, 38(6): 729–745. DOI: 10.1080/02614367.2019.1662830.

Ma, S. C., & Kaplanidou, K. (2021). Social capital and running: A network social capital perspective. *Sustainability*, 13(22), 12398.

Mair, J., Chien, P.M., Kelly, S.J., & Derrington, S. (2021). Social impacts of mega-events: A systematic narrative review and research agenda. *Journal of Sustainable Tourism*, 1–22. DOI: 10.1080/09669582.2020.1870989

Mazzucato, M. (2018). *The value of everything*. Milton Keynes: Allen Lane.

Meynhardt, T. (2009). Public value inside: What is public value creation?. *International Journal of Public Administration*, 32(3–4): 192–219.

Meynhardt, T. (2015). Public value: Turning a conceptual framework into a scorecard. In J.M. Bryson, B.C. Crosby & L. Bloomberg (Eds.), *Public value and public administration* (pp. 147–169). Washington, DC: Georgetown University Press.

Misener, L. (2015). Leveraging parasport events for community participation: Development of a theoretical framework. *European Sport Management Quarterly*, 15(1): 132–153.

Neri, M.C. (Ed.). (2020). *Evaluating the local impacts of the Rio Olympics*. London: Routledge.

Ohmann, S., Jones, I., & Wilkes, K. (2006). The perceived social impacts of the 2006 Football World Cup on Munich residents. *Journal of Sport & Tourism*, 11: 129–152.

Olberding, J.C., & Olberding, D.J. (2014). The social impacts of a special event on the host city: A conceptual framework and a case study of the Cincinnati Flying Pig Marathon. *International Journal of Hospitality and Event Management*, 1(1): 44–61.

Peric, M., Đurkin, J., & Wise, N. (2016). Leveraging small-scale sport events: Challenges of organising, delivering and managing sustainable outcomes

in rural communities, the case of Gorski Kotar, Croatia. *Sustainability*, *8*(12): 1337. DOI: 10.3390/su8121337.
Pfitzner, R., & Koenigstorfer, J. (2017). Corporate running event participation improves organizational climate in employees. *Journal of Global Sport Management*, *2*(4): 275–292.
Preuss, H. (2015). A framework for identifying the legacies of a mega sport event. *Leisure Studies*, *34*(6): 627–642.
Ritchie, J.R. (1984). Assessing the impact of hallmark events: Conceptual and research issues. *Journal of Travel Research*, *23*(1): 2–11. DOI: 10.1177/004728758402300101.
Scheu, A., Preuß, H., & K€onecke, T. (2021). The legacy of the Olympic games: A review. *Journal of Global Sport Management*, *6*(3): 212–233. DOI: 10.1080/24704067.2019.1566757.
Schneider, P.P., Smith, R.A., Bullas, A.M., Bayley, T., Haake, S.S.J., Brennan, A., & Goyder, E. (2019). Where should new parkrun events be located? Modelling the potential impact of 200 new events on socio-economic inequalities in access and participation. *medRxiv* 2019: 19004143.
Schneider, P.P., Smith, R.A., Bullas, A.M., Quirk, H., Bayley, T., Haake, S.J., Brennan, A., & Goyder, E. (2020). Multiple deprivation and geographic distance to community physical activity events — achieving equitable access to parkrun in England. *Public Health*, *189*: 48–53. DOI: 10.1016/j.puhe.2020.09.002.
Snow, D., & Benford, R. (1988). Ideology, frame resonance and participant mobilization. *International Social Movements Research*, *1*: 197–218.
Surborg, B., VanWynsberghe, R., & Wyly, E. (2008). Mapping the Olympic growth machine: Transnational urbanism and the growth machine diaspora. *City*, *12*(3): 341–355.
Taks, M., Chalip, L., & Green, B.C. (2015). Impacts and strategic outcomes from non-mega sport events for local communities. *European Sport Management Quarterly*, *15*(1): 1–6.
Teare, G., & Taks, M. (2021). Sport events for sport participation: A scoping review. *Frontiers in Sports and Active Living*, 19 May 2021. DOI: 10.3389/fspor.2021.655579.
Temerak, M.S., & Winklhofer, H. (2021). Participant engagement in running events and why it matters who else takes part. *European Sport Management Quarterly*. DOI: 10.1080/16184742.2021.1956990.
Thomson, A., Cuskelly, G., Toohey, K., Kennelly, M., Burton, P., & Fredline, L. (2018). Sport event legacy: A systematic quantitative review of literature. *Sport Management Review*, *22*(3): 295–321. DOI: 10.1016/j.smr.2018.06.011.
Wallstam, M., Ioannides, D., & Pettersson, R. (2020). Evaluating the social impacts of events: In search of unified indicators for effective policymaking. *Journal of Policy Research in Tourism, Leisure and Events*, *12*(2): 122–141. DOI: 10.1080/19407963.2018.1515214.
Xing, X., & Chen, S. (2021). Beijing 2008: One world, one dream. In *Sport Participation and Olympic Legacies* (pp. 79–104). Routledge.

Xing, X., Zhang, R., & Taks, M. (2022). The effects of health, social, and consumption capital on running-related expenditures in China. *European Sport Management Quarterly*, *22*(3), 398–418.

Zhou, R., Kaplanidou, K., & Wegner, C. (2021). Social capital from sport event participation: Scale development and validation. *Leisure Studies*, *40*(5): 612–627. DOI: 10.1080/02614367.2021.1916832.

Zimbalist, A. (2015). *Circus maximus: The economic gamble behind hosting the Olympics and the World Cup*. Washington, DC: Brookings Institution Press.

Case study 4.1 The LifeSouth race weekend, Gainesville, Florida

Kyriaki Kaplanidou

Running events have grown in popularity in the United States, especially short-distance events like 5k. To be more specific, and according to runningintheusa.com there were about 22,560 5k running events taking place in all 51 states during 2021. Typically, 5k events take place in combination with half-marathons or marathons. A combination of these events includes a 5-km event and a half-marathon which are held during the Life South Race Weekend, in the city of Gainesville, Florida. These events are an initiative of the LifeSouth Community Foundation (formerly Five Points of Life). The LifeSouth Community Foundation provides education to K-12 students about the need for blood donation and the event participants become part of this cause. The event is also important for the local community and city of Gainesville, Florida, as this organisation is local and provides the opportunity to local people to have a race weekend in their city.

Running event history

The LifeSouth Race weekend consists of a 5k, half-marathon, and Kids' Marathon, as well as a fitness expo. This event attracts runners from inside and outside the state of Florida. This portfolio of races over the weekend is in its 16th year. Before the portfolio of events was named LifeSouth Race Weekend, there was one main running event, which was called the five points of life marathon, but it included also a half-marathon. According to the organisers, the race offers opportunity to runners to experience the city of Gainesville and also through their registration to donate towards initiatives that create awareness about blood donations. The race passes by all the major landmarks the city of Gainesville offers and makes the course more interesting to run. It is also the only race weekend in the city of Gainesville that offers the opportunity to local residents to run in a local half-marathon. The importance of the charity is undoubtable, which is evident in the support of the local businesses. In fact, there are 12 local sponsor companies that support this race weekend.

These include local organisations such as super markets, hospitals, banks, restaurants, insurance companies, and automotive companies. As noted by the organisers, "our business and charity partners ensure that runners are provided a premium race experience, with beautiful and secured courses, exceptional amenities, and a blockbuster post-race experience" (Lifesouth Community Foundation, 2022a). The event organisers provide recognition awards to the 1st, 2nd and 3rd place finishers for each race type. There is also a post event street festival that offers food and live entertainment to the participants. Due to the scale of the sport event, there is no media interest besides the local newspaper that covers the event. The event is logistically supported from the Gainesville Sport Commission, an organisation whose main mission is to boost sport tourism in the County where they operate, specifically, in this case, Alachua County, in the state of Florida.

Running event aims, ownership, geography and participants

The purpose of the LifeSouth Race Weekend race is to meet the needs of patients through increasing awareness among current and future generations about the importance of blood donation. Specifically, they want to raise a 'Donation Generation' of young people who understand and are committed to giving the gift of life. As the organisers say, there's no substitute for human blood, and donations provide relief and hope for patients with life-threatening diseases and trauma victims. LifeSouth is the local blood centre, and the only provider of blood and blood products to the major hospitals in the Gainesville area and more than a hundred other hospitals throughout Florida, Georgia and Alabama. Gainesville, as the host city, is a college city that has a population of approximately 132,000 people. Gainesville also is the host city for one of the biggest hospitals in the state of Florida. Gainesville is located in the middle of the state of Florida and it is two hours driving distance from major cities, such as Jacksonville, Orlando and Tampa. The total number of race participants including the 5k runs reached up to 1,500.

The half-marathon race course goes through the downtown of the city which features attractions such as a park with a pond, and a local theatre. The event has been sanctioned by the USA Track and Field federation. The early registration fee is $80 (US dollars) and the late registration fee is 90$ (US dollars). In a personal communication with the event organisers in 2016, they provided a strength, weakness, opportunities and threats (SWOT) analysis about their events. The strengths included the strong cause associated with the events, a variety of races available to runners, well-funded marketing efforts and partnerships with large and reputable companies. The weaknesses included not targeting the running market properly, low social media presence, the physical layout of the course (which since 2016 has changed) and the existence of a time limit to finish the race. Opportunities were other thriving health and fitness organisations in the area, the large student population body coming from the University of Florida located in Gainesville, a strong University Athletic department and University willingness to support large donors with various perks. Threats were the weather and other similar events in the region. The event organisers also indicated that their target markets includes two types. The first one targeted white upper class males with strong work ethic and goals between the ages of 35 and 55. This market was selected in order to achieve larger donations for the Foundation. The second type targeted college students from middle to upper class backgrounds with a desire to compete and make a difference. The event organisers evaluated the event using their own surveys and also monitored the number and amount of participants and donations achieved over the years.

Running event organisation

The event is organised by LifeSouth Community Foundation in very close collaboration and support from the Gainesville Sport Commission. According to their website:

> The Gainesville Sports Commission (GSC) founded in 1988, is a not-for-profit organization that strives to promote tourism through sports while creating a positive economic impact on Gainesville and Alachua county. The Gainesville Sports Commission is a liaison that brings sporting events to our local community and assists with hosting, creating

and supporting over 45 events annually. Since its inception, Gainesville Sports Commission has directly contributed more than 300 million dollars of economic growth. By bringing participants and spectators to sporting events, Gainesville Sports Commission creates approximately 20 million dollars annually of direct economic impact for our community.
(Gainesville Sports Commission, n.d.)

The event is promoted by the LifeSouth Community Foundation through their website and their social media presence in Facebook which has 3,000 people who like their page. This is where the Foundation is also promoting the results of the race along with race highlights and other information material (LifeSouth Community Foundation, 2022b). In 2022, there were about 1,400 running event participants.

LifeSouth Run impacts

As Kaplanidou (2020) explained, sport events can be viewed as contributors to community development in various ways. The most obvious one is the economic contribution small-scale sport events can have on the community due to the influx of tourists to the area, small-scale sport events can contribute also to social change, social issue management and social capital development, if managed properly. One aspect that is also part of a community development is the improvement of human capital which small-scale sport events can offer to younger population through opportunities for volunteering. Furthermore, the networks build during the preparation and participation in these events can increase social capital and therefore contribute to social impacts (Zhou & Kaplanidou, 2018). But equally important, is the how small-scale events by not building new venues and wasting resources can help the environmental protection of a host region. All these goals certainly correlate with improving the quality of life of local people.

When it comes to data about the running event presented in this study, there was evidence among the participants of this event about the high level of intangible impacts on their quality of life (among other concepts). Specifically, during a survey that was performed with the participants of the event in 2016, it was found that participating in the event influenced the majority of the participants' quality of life perceptions, as well as what they are achieving in life, the quality of their personal relationships and their standard of living. The sample consisted from participants with an average age of about 43 years old, most participants (about 57%) earned above $80,000, were married (about 62%), were highly educated with a college degree of advanced college degree (about 88%) and where white (83.7%). Most of the participants were avid event participants with an average participation number between two and three running events per year. The majority of the participants (65.6%) had spent between $101 and $500 for event registration fees during the past 12 months from the day of the survey. In addition, slightly less than 40% of the participants travelled more than 80 km to attend the event.

Furthermore, from the same data set, the Life South Race weekend running increased the quality of social life, feelings of safety and community connections, as well as the participants' perceptions of future security and work life. In addition, the participants were highly satisfied and happy with their decision to participate in the Life South Race event. Interestingly, 81% of the survey participants indicated that the participation in all the running sport events they have had so far in their life contributed to their life happiness. The race also contributed to the more than a third of the participants' achievement of getting a wider social network within or outside a running group (about 37%). The race participation also provided recognition of achievement among family and work colleagues for most participants (59%). Equally interesting, most of the survey participants (about 59%) indicated they would participate again in the event in the following year. Most importantly, the event contributed a lot to the participants' happiness in life (about 82%) but most interestingly, participation in a portfolio of running events contributed to the participants' happiness in life (about 96%).

These results suggest how small-scale running events can boost quality of life perceptions and become an anchor for better living conditions in a community that hosts them. The improvement of quality of life and also the feelings of happiness the participants felt are intangible psychological event impacts.

The achievement of social network expansion related to notions of social capital and therefore social impacts. Furthermore, the intent of most people to participate again in the race suggests the likely tangible economic impacts via tourism development.

The data presented above suggest how smaller scale sport events can really contribute to a small-sized community and also to the quality of life of the local people. Since running events are offered in abundance in the United States and every area features their own running event that has witnessed growth over the years, it is important to consider how running, as an activity, can really contribute to efforts of community development.

References

Gainesville Sports Commission. (n.d.). About Us. Retrieved April 5, 2022, from htttps://www.gainesvillesportscommission.com/about-us/

Kaplanidou, K. (2020). Sport events and community development: Resident considerations and community goals. *International Journal of Sports Marketing and Sponsorship, ahead of print.* doi: DOI: 10.1108/IJSMS-05-2020-0082.

Lifesouth Community Foundation. (2022a) Retrieved April 5, 2022, from https://www.lifesouthcommunityfoundation.org

LifeSouth Community Foundation. (2022b). Facebook Page. Retrieved April 5, 2022, from https://www.facebook.com/LifeSouthCommunityFoundation

Zhou, R., & Kaplanidou, K. (2018). Building social capital from sport event participation: An exploration of the social impacts of participatory sport events on the community. *Sport Management Review, 21*(5): 491–503. DOI: 10.1016/j.smr.2017.11.001

Case study 4.2 Running events in China and their impact

Xiaoyan Xing and Yue Liu

This case study illustrates the sheer number and types of running events in China. It takes a broader view of running events' impacts by connecting them to national and local policies and strategic governance.

The rise of running events: the precursor to impact

The Beijing Marathon was the first city marathon in China. Initially attended by only 86 elite runners from 12 countries in 1981, it expanded to become a mass participatory sport event only at the turn of the millennium, when it included shorter races (e.g., half-marathons, 10-km races) that attracted thousands of amateur runners (Zhang, 2021). Nonetheless, approximately 10 more years would pass before China experienced its nationwide running boom. Figure 4.1 shows that the number of running events

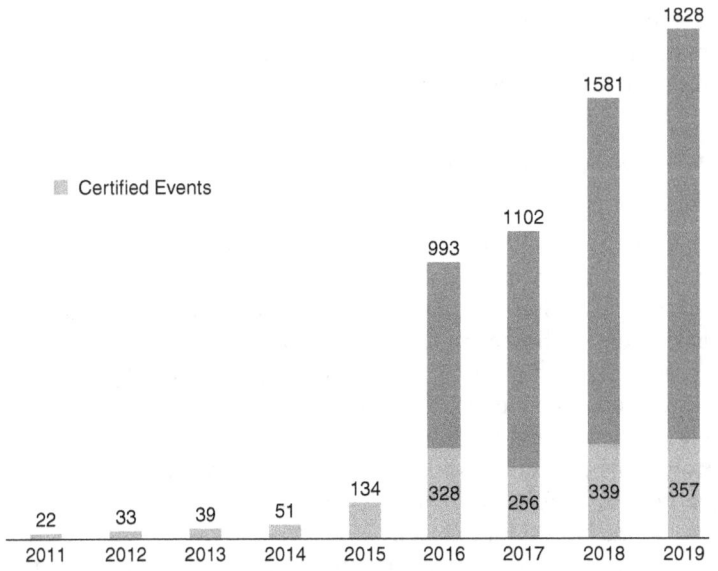

Figure 4.1 Number of running events in China.

certified by the CAA (Chinese Athletic Association) increased from 22 in 2011 to 357 in 2019, with the largest surge in 2015. Similarly, the total number of sizable events[1] (including certified events) increased from 993 in 2016 to 1,828 in 2019 (not including Macao, Hong Kong or Taiwan; CAA, 2020).

Multiple factors contributed to China's running boom in the 2010s. The per capita GDP in China surpassed US$5,000 in 2011 and US$10,000 in 2019 (National Bureau of Statistics of China, 2020), providing a solid economic base for leisure and sport consumption. China's growing middle-class, seeking health and happiness, were largely responsible for that consumption (Xing et al., 2020). They favoured running not only because it was accessible but also because, as a lifestyle sport, running projected a positive self-image. Public figures such as business leaders and journalists were early adopters. They travelled internationally to compete for the Six Star Medal at the WMMs (World Marathon Majors) and posted their experiences on then-nascent social media (i.e., the miniblog named Weibo and WeChat),[2] promoting running events to the public, attracting millions more people to attend other running events, and creating social impact in the process. Running subsequently proliferated in China because many serious runners there enthused about the sport and promoted it among their peers.

Policy and governance impacts

China's policy approach of fostering new economic growth through sport and stimulating consumption through mass sport participation in the early 2010s (Xing & Chen, 2021) propelled multiple stakeholders (i.e., local governments, venture capitalists, and entrepreneurs) to stage running events. For local governments, city marathons achieved multiple policy objectives by showcasing their cities as tourist destinations, demonstrating city achievements through reform, promoting mass sport, and bolstering the sport industry. This trend soon caught on. By the end of 2019, 89.2% of China's 337 municipalities held their own city marathons (CAA, 2020).

The sport industry attracted major capital due to the favourable policy environment promised in the 2014 State Council–issued document entitled *Opinions on Accelerating the*

Development of the Sport Industry and Promoting Sport Consumption, which has since been widely considered the primary policy document relating to China's sport industry (Zheng et al., 2019). Major national companies such as Alibaba (IT), Suning (retail) and Wanda (real estate) swiftly responded to the policy call by diversifying into the area of sport through the acquisition of various sport- and running-related intellectual property. For instance, Wanda acquired *Infront*, a global sport and media company, in 2015 and signed a strategic agreement with the WMMs in 2017. Alibaba Sport secured the organising rights for the 2018–2021 Hangzhou Marathon with an unusual offer of more than CNY¥1 billion (US$ 220 million) to the owner of the event rights, and the offer was so high because the bidding was extremely competitive. At the same time, avid runners, typically with IT, media, and business backgrounds, created their own running-related businesses just as the state was calling for 'mass entrepreneurship and innovation' (i.e., individuals building their own innovative business enterprises), starting with Premier Li Keqiang's speech at the 2014 Summer Davos in Tianjin, China (Li, 2014).

Thusly, incited by the national government, various stakeholders considered the social and economic potential of running events. The events' social impacts (i.e., running improved health and happiness among middle-class people) were leveraged for economic gains. A prominent policy document titled *Development Plan for the Marathon Sport Industry* – issued in 2017 by the GAS (General Administration of Sport) and the National Development and Reform Commission along with nine government ministries (GAS, 2017) – clarified the policy approach whereby participation in running events was to be fostered to create economic growth.

Finally, the popularisation of running in the 2010s is attributable to solid governance by the CAA. The association formed a road race commission, comprising mainly members of provincial marathon associations and industry representatives. By developing a participant database using statistics from the CAA's certified running events, the organisation was able to announce running statistics for the year at its annual marathon conference before the COVID-19 pandemic. In addition, the CAA's running event management provided specific instructions to ensure safety during running events (e.g., risk management, penalties and procedures for rule violations and doping prevention); how-to guides were offered for staging of and participation in running events (including virtual races). Most importantly, the CAA outlined requirements for race organisation, race certification, race prizes, event company certification, regulations for the agents of elite runners, and so on (CAA, 2022). Notably, the CAA succeeded in developing such a governance structure for running events from scratch at a time when the GAS was struggling to 'unhook' its NSOs (National Sporting Organisations), including the Chinese Football Association, and produce 'independent' social organisations subject to less government intervention. The CAA's success in establishing itself during the running boom was considered an exemplar for other NSOs.

Impacts on the organisation of running events

A panoramic view of running event organisation in China helps to explain these events' social and economic impacts. For a better understanding, we selected statistics from 2019 (CAA, 2020) as an example because the COVID-19 pandemic later hampered the running industry severely.

Event types. The 1,828 running events held in 2019 included on average 3,898 participants each, and more than 700 million participant times in total. The CAA categorised running events according to their longest race; as such, a marathon event could also include half-marathons, 10-km races, or 5-km races. The most popular event types in 2019 were trail runs (481 events; on mountain/hill terrains), followed by half-marathons (467 events; on city roads or parks), mini runs (337 events; mainly in parks), and then marathons (249 events; on city roads) (CAA, 2020).

Certification. The certified events held in 2019 typically had numerous participants. The 357 CAA-certified running events averaged 11,874 participants and accounted for nearly 60% of all running event participation in 2019. Events with top-level CAA certification were then eligible to apply for status as a WA (World Athletics) Label road race. Twenty-four marathons in China achieved WA Label status in 2019, rendering China the country with the most WA Label road races (followed by Spain and Japan). Furthermore, 14 marathons obtained certification from the Association of International Marathons and Distance Races in 2019 (CAA, 2020).

Ownership, organisers and government support. The hosting rights of marathons and half-marathons in China are usually owned by city governments, whereas the hosting rights for trail runs and other event types are mostly owned by event companies. Regardless of who owns the hosting rights, most running events (including marathons and half-marathons) are organised by domestic event companies. Typically, formal bids to organise city marathons are placed by local sport bureaus on behalf of their cities, and contract lengths ranges from one to eight years. Major national event companies secure organising rights to multiple city marathons nationwide. Nonetheless, organising a city marathon in China is unprofitable except in major cities such as Beijing, Shanghai and Xiamen, which attract major sponsorships. As such, local governments provide significant compensation to ensure that event companies winning bids at least break even. Local governments also provide support such as road closures, security and public transport services for marathon staging.

Participants, accessibility and geographical coverage. The city marathons in China attract mainly Chinese amateur runners at the regional and national levels. More than 900,000 participants completed at least one CAA-certified half-marathon or marathon event in 2019 (CAA, 2020). Over 80% of these participants were aged 30 years or older, and the gender split was 75% to 25% male to female. Running event registration is easily affordable. For example, the registration fees for the 2019 Shanghai and Beijing marathons were CNY¥100 (US$ 15) and CNY¥200 (US$ 30), respectively. However, these events were extremely popular. Participants entered a draw to obtain a spot. The chance of gaining one of the 30,000 entries for the 2019 Beijing Marathon was only 16%. At the other end of the spectrum, most newly established city marathons struggled to recruit enough participants. Nonetheless, even top city marathons in China failed to attract many participants from abroad or to secure large spectator crowds along the race courses. The rare exceptions were courses that had notable tourist attractions and for which special efforts were devoted to marketing that would attract international runners, such as in the case of the Great Wall Marathon.

Prizes. To encourage participation and incentivise record-setting, most marathon events offered prize money. Although most races had fewer than 30 elite runners, the prizes even attracted Kenyan runners recruited and trained by Chinese agents. Similarly, a few top Chinese amateur runners turned professional to earn prize money. This phenomenon prompted the CAA to cap prize money for running events. For instance, the top prize for a WA Gold Label race now cannot exceed US$45,000 (CAA, 2022).

Auxiliary events and activities. Exhibitions positioned either near the course or in a location of the organisers' choosing were typically established where participants congregated before and/or on the race day. A two-to-three-day exhibition offered promotional opportunities for sponsors, tourist attractions, and producers of local specialties as well as activities such as running workshops, press conferences, and interviews with or chances to meet elite runners and pacers. Created by the CAA in 2016, the China Marathon Expo was the largest exhibition of its kind in the country. It was held annually in conjunction with the Xiamen Marathon – one of the earliest marathons in China effectively used for destination marketing. Some city marathons also included short family runs and breakfast runs to increase marketing exposure for sponsors and social opportunities for participants.

As mentioned, Chinese local governments held running events mainly to generate social and economic impacts. To this end, some cities staged sport industry summits or business leader forums around event times. A so-called race-inside-the-race was sometimes used to entice potential business investors to visit the city. Finally, major city marathons typically featured a charity component to support various charitable causes. However, while charity runs had been increasing over the years, they were far less pervasive than in the West.

Media coverage. Extensive media reporting around running events and host cities not only benefitted tourism but also showcased local governments' achievements in terms of reform. As such, city marathons usually had an extensive media matrix, including an event website, official social media accounts and partnerships with print and online media at the local, regional and even national levels. Controversially, local government officials were keen for their marathons to be broadcast live on China's national television channels to achieve the aforementioned policy objectives despite low viewing figures and high broadcasting fees. In fact, these television broadcasting fees were one of the largest expenditures for city marathons.

Formal evaluation. Post-event participant surveys were conducted for approximately 40% of running events in 2019 and event impacts assessed for 30% (Chengguangxian, 2020). These evaluations, either conducted by the event company itself or commissioned to a third party, assessed event media coverage, event service quality and runners' tourism expenditure during events. Findings revealed that a tourist runner at a newly established city marathon spent an average of CNY¥1,139 (US$ 171) at the destination in 2019. This average expenditure increased to CNY¥3,771 (US$ 565) at the Chengdu Marathon, which was eligible to become a WMM race and had an established event brand in a city with abundant tourist attractions (Xing et al., 2022). Overall, major city marathons in China provided more positive social and economic contributions to their host cities than did most other major sport events. In an impact evaluation of the top 12 sport events held in Shanghai in 2019, the economic impact of the Shanghai Marathon, which amounted to CNY¥1.47 billion (US$ 220.3 million), ranked third only behind the F1 Chinese Grand Prix and the Shanghai Masters (Sina, 2020).

Running events during the COVID-19 pandemic and its 'impact on impacts'

The COVID-19 pandemic drastically hindered the growth of running events in China. Few city marathons happened in late 2020, and some were cancelled at the last minute because of COVID-19, even when tourist runners had already arrived at the destination. Almost all city marathons were halted in 2021, and the 2022 Omicron outbreak again dampened hopes of recovery. With small event companies disappearing and large ones struggling financially, China's running industry was in jeopardy. The CAA adopted several measures to mitigate the pandemic's effects. Notably, the organisation collaborated with sport bureaus nationwide to launch the *Running China Online Marathon Series* in 2020, resulting in 435 virtual races held over two years with more than a million participant times (CAA, 2022). However, the aforementioned numbers paled in comparison with those for running events in 2019. More significantly, the 2022 CAA policy initiative encouraged frequent, small-scale, short-distance running events with both offline and virtual forms to comply with the many pandemic-related restrictions on event organisation (CAA, 2022). However, the rapid development of running events in China during the 2010s was spearheaded by large-scale city marathons. Academics criticised the lack of grassroots running events for building participation during the running boom. The incentive of completing a city marathon as a personal achievement also caused inadequate training and frequent injuries among participants (Xing et al., 2022). The CAA's new approach may somewhat address such problems. Nevertheless, the question remains as to whether this strategic adaptation to pandemic conditions will help China's running industry to survive into the post-COVID era.

Notes

1 A statistic formulated by the CAA in 2016. A sizable running event must have a minimum of 800 participants for road races and 300 for trail or mountain runs.
2 The explosive increase of social media users in China happened in early 2010s. For instance, WeChat was launched in January 2011 and reached 600 million users in October 2013.

References

CAA. (2020). *2019 Chinese marathon blue book*. Beijing: The Author.
CAA. (2022). *CAA's compilation of road race management documents*. https://www.runchina.org.cn/#/news/news-detail/XW20220271
Chengguangxian. (2020). *Report of the 2019 national running event management survey*. https://mp.weixin.qq.com/s/tFvm-xTrHtHLZF2eSZCy-A
GAS. (2017). *Development plan of the marathon sport industry*. Beijing: The Author.
Li, K. (2014). *Li's Speech at the 2014 Summer Davos*. http://www.gov.cn/guowuyuan/2014-09/11/content_2748703.htm
National Bureau of Statistics of China. (2020). *2020 China statistics year book*. http://www.stats.gov.cn/tjsj/ndsj/2020/indexch.htm

Sina. (2020). *Shanghai Marathon scoring 1.47 billion economic impact.* http://sports.sina.com.cn/run/2020-06-05/doc-iirczymk5339092.shtml

Xing, X., Yan, M., & You, Y. (2022). How to attract consumption through hosting a marathon. *Leisure Sports and Health*, 2(1): 1–11.

Xing, X., Zhang, R., Wang, J., & Bai, J. (2020). Effects of scientific training attitude, training and competition on RRIs. *China Sport Science and Technology*, 58(4): 81–89.

Zhang, L. (2021). *China's marathon era.* Beijing: Electronic Industry Press.

Zheng, J., Chen, S., Tan, T., & Houlihan, B. (2019). *Sport policy in China.* London: Routledge.

5 Conclusion

Vassil Girginov

Introduction

Running's transitioning from the athletic track to city streets, parks and nature in the late 1960s and 1970s has been closely intertwined with broader political, social and economic agendas. The popularity of running has earned it the status of a dedicated Global Running Day held on the first Wednesday of June each year. While running continues to be an individual pursuit where runners create their own social worlds (Shipway et al., 2013), it also possesses the power to bring diverse people and communities together. Currently, the popular initiative 'Park Run' welcomes every Sunday morning people from all walks of life and abilities in 22 countries around the world for a friendly 5k run. One does not need anything to participate apart from a pair of trainers and knowledge about the location and time of the run. For example, in 2022, the UK Park Run alone reports some 770 locations with 40, 211,857 finishers and 7,465 organised groups. These impressive figures could not have been achieved without the support of an army of some 355,791 volunteers (https://www.parkrun.org.uk/), which is another measure of the popularity and social impact of this form of running.

The transitioning of running from an exclusive to an egalitarian pursuit is not simply a historical fact but a social and political process as well. The repositioning of the New York Marathon (NYM) is a case in point. The first edition of the NYM in 1970 was a male affair attracting some 127 avid runners (only one woman competed but did not finish the race) in Central Park with an entry fee of $1 and a budget of $1,000. In the space of 50 years, the NYM has become a mass event with over 50,000 participants that is open for women, sponsors and TV deals and marked by the accompanying processes of commercialisation, democratisation and spectacularisation. The economic impact of

DOI: 10.4324/9781003301691-5

Conclusion 133

the NYM in 2017 was $415 million with additional expected sales and occupancy taxes of $22.2 million and was watched by some 2.5 million spectators. This high-profile running event has also raised $270 million since the start of the Official Charity Partner Program in 2006 (Martin & Hall, 2020). But the transition from elite to egalitarian did not happen smoothly. Rather, it involved a great deal of advocacy, lobbying and political action. In the 1970s, competitive amateur sport in America was governed by the American Athletic Union (AAU) whose rules forbid women from competing in races longer than 1.5 miles. When the AAU finally allowed women to participate in the NYM in 1971, it was on the condition that they would start 10 minutes earlier than men. Then at the start of the 1971 marathon when the gun went off, the women, led by their most prominent advocate Nina Kuscsik, staged a protest, sat down and held up signs which read: "Hey, AAU. This is 1972. Wake up" (Crawford, 2021). Not only had sport-governing bodies to wake up to the social and economic potential of running, but equally public authorities, businesses and the research community. This process has been constantly invigorating itself by turning running into a social movement or integrating it with existing ones such as providing support for good causes, raising public awareness about health and inequality and more recently, by contributing to sustainable development.

From Couch to 5k: the politics, marketing and impact of running events

The history of running has always been associated with some utilitarian purposes, including survival, fitness for warfare, community building and health. Thus, as a form of human behaviour, running has an inherent and universal political appeal that can be evoked in various contexts. 'From Couch to 5k' is a typical example of turning running into a policy issue by incorporating it in the work of the biggest national and highly politically charged organisation in the UK, the National Health Service (NHS). NHS promotes 'From Couch to 5k', which is a running plan for absolute beginners and offers support for those wishing to change their behaviour and gain some health benefits (https://www.nhs.uk/live-well/exercise/running-and-aerobic-exercises/get-running-with-couch-to-5k/).

The purposeful and multimodal nature of running illustrates well its political dimension. As demonstrated by the analysis of 12 running events in this book, as well as other studies, the primary objective of most running events is no longer to determine the winners of different distances but to address wider policy issues such as health, social inclusion, city regeneration and sustainability. While the contribution of sport events to raising public awareness is well-established, charging one day running event with a multitude of social and political objectives has become a challenge for their identity, management and impacts. Running events' objectives are closely intertwined to their identity and are critical for their success. All studied events claim a rather broad range of objectives, including promoting health, fitness, education, community spirit, supporting good causes and providing fun and entertainment, among others. They also cater for broader audiences and try to accommodate diverse groups of people, including children, families, competitive and recreational runners, and people with disabilities. Some of the audiences will be driven mainly by the 'competitive' impulse, while other would be interested in 'completing' the race. Naturally, the focus of the event and its objectives will have ramifications for the event offer and impact on different audiences.

Herrick's (2015) insightful analysis of two mass participation running events held in the north of England (the Great North Run, Newcastle, GNR) and in Addis Ababa, the capital of Ethiopia (The Great Ethiopian Run, GER), demonstrates how running can be **manufactured** to serve two different policy objectives and to produce different impacts. The GNR was framed as having public health relevance and as a significant boost to Newcastle's urban and regional regeneration. In contrast, the GER's prime objective was to raise awareness of HIV/AIDS and the Millennium Development Goals. Similar to GNR, GER has also been harnessed for image-building purposes of the capital city and Ethiopia more generally. Interestingly, both running events have been connected through Nova International, a marketing company specialising in organising mass participation events. The broader political point for Herrick (2015, p. 299) is that "MPREs (*mass participation running events, explanation added*) thus represent a particular form of 'urban spectacle' 'that involve[s] capitalist markets, sets of social relations, and flows of commodities, capital, technology, cultural forms and people across borders' (Gotham, 2005: 227)".

The manufacturing of running has become a profitable enterprise for a host of organisations nationally and internationally. This has increased events' complexity and institutional regulation, including their certification by professional bodies such as World Athletics (WA) or the Association of International Marathons and Distance Races (AIMDR). In 2022, the AIMRD has 442-member races in 120 countries around the world (https://aims-worldrunning.org/directory.html).

Conclusion   135

Adding running events to local authorities' and national sport organisations' calendars has provided them with extra legitimacy and institutional support. Another implication of the standardisation of running events manufacturing has been the raising expectations of participants, spectators and stakeholders. To obtain a certification, an event must meet a range of technical, security, safety, environmental, financial and impact requirements. With heightened expectations come greater challenges for event organisers, which makes running events **contested** on the grounds of their location, competition with existing events, ability to deliver positive and to minimise negative impacts for individuals and communities. Alexandris et al. (2017) examined the link between event quality and loyalty of runners and note that the service environment and outcome dimensions contributed significantly to the prediction of event loyalty. Peckover et al. (2022) documented the negative impact of running events congestion on participants' satisfaction. As elaborated in Chapter 3 (marketing), establishing a coherent event concept, which captures the broader policy objectives of organisers, and its subsequent communication to different target groups is critical.

Charging running events with a multitude of policy objectives creates challenges for the conceptualisation and documentation of their promotion and impacts. Three interrelated issues pertinent to events policy (i.e., visions), marketing and impacts deserve attention. The first issue concerns the running event offer, which refers to the specific exchange that participants enter in with event organisers. It is different from the event objectives but closely complements them and the exchange may take a tangible (e.g., paying a registration fee and receiving a service pack) or intangible (e.g., one gains self-confidence and pride in exchange of their time and support for the event) form. Naturally, the event offer needs to be made relevant to different target groups. The events examined in this book did have an offer but it has not always been clearly spelled out. General offers such as 'join us and have fun' resonate differently with different target groups and usually do not deliver the desired results.

The second issue stems directly from the first one and involves the need to clearly identify the event public. This is important for two main reasons, including our ability to determine the nature of ensuing interactions and what has been exchanged in the process. Event interactions always take place between an individual and the event and the value of the event can only be established based on personal perceptions and experiences. Striking a balance between events broader policy objectives and the needs of various target groups such as children, adults, athletes, recreational participants and stakeholders remains very challenging. Regarding the exchange process stimulated by the event, five main resources could be involved, including moral, cultural, socio-organisational, human and material (Edwards & Gillham, 2013), all of which will have a bearing on participants' experiences and the overall event impact.

The third issue concerns our understanding of the production of running events impacts. It brings together the event offer, and the interactions generated by it under the notion of public value. The main premise of the concept of public value is that it represents a relationship between a valuing subject (i.e., a runner, spectator and stakeholder) and valued object (i.e., the running event itself). As discussed above, due to conceptual and methodological challenges in documenting intangible impacts, events promoters tend to focus on the tangibles and use them for promotional and resource-generation purposes. Without exception, all running events have much greater stated intangible impacts such as healthy lifestyle benefits, which directly correlates with their broader well-being objectives. But these intangible impacts represent aggregates, which unless translated into specific individual perceptions and experience will remain exactly that, aggregates. After all, public value is always in the eye of the beholder.

Comprehensive studies on running events' impacts are a rarity, which in the era of evidence-based policy making (Cairney, 2016) creates a gulf between their proclaimed objectives and actual documented benefits. None of the 12 events studied ever had their impact evaluated, save some limited feedback from participants and social media analyses. Therefore, no conclusive answer to the question 'how promises of impact are delivered and at what cost?' can be provided. The reasons for the lack of impact evaluations are multiple but they boil down to the lack of political will, expertise and resources. Nonetheless, as demonstrated by some of the case studies in this book, the visions for running events impacts can come from local leaders (i.e., LifeSouth Race Weekend) as well as from broader political decisions aimed at establishing the conditions necessary to deliver the impacts (i.e., China's running boom). Whatever the case, the three key tasks of framing running events and their impacts have been at work (Snow & Benford, 1988). The diagnostic framing in the case of LifeSouth Race Weekend allowed the organisers to position blood donation as a lifesaving activity worthy of support. The diagnostic frame was then connected to the prognostic frame, which formulated the expected impacts from participation in the event such as the sense of pride and accomplishment, community building and contributing to the common good. Finally, the organisers deployed the motivational frame to convince people and stakeholders to participate.

China used a different diagnostic frame concerned with health, social development and economic prosperity. The prognostic frame, although not explicitly formulated as an expected impact but as a policy outcome, was designed to encourage public and private entrepreneurship, which, in turn, has provided the social and economic motivational frame for individuals and organisations to embrace running.

Studying running events

Returning to Handelman's (1998) question posed in the introductory chapter 'why study public events', this book provides support for his answer that "events are important phenomena because they constitute a dense concentration of symbols and their associations are of relevance to particular people" (p. 9). The events examined by this book as well as by other studies offer ample evidence for the relevance of running to individuals, organisations and places across various socio-economic contexts. The heuristic device provided by Handelman for understanding events as models and mirrors allows further unpacking their significance for people and societies from a macro perspective.

Handelman (1998) was writing mainly about traditional festivals, and the present study has revealed that among the 12 running events investigated, the BoslandTrail (Belgium) could be classed as a model because it was set up with the explicit objective to challenge the 'existing order' and to offer a model of ecologically friendly running. Although the remaining 11 events served more as a mirror of societies where they were held (i.e., heritage events and promoting urban regeneration), many of them were not necessarily a clear-cut fit. This is because several events have been breaking the mould by including elements of 'the model' such as promoting sustainable behaviour and technological innovations or more broadly connecting previously unrelated life experiences as in the case of connecting spirituality, nature and sport through ultra-trail races (Botella-Carrubi et al., 2019).

The running events typology developed in Chapter 1 provides a conceptual device for investigation based on a logical move between events' policy properties (i.e., ownership, form and function), promotion (i.e., location, participants and side activities) and impacts (i.e., organiser, access and participants). In this way, it becomes possible for the analysis to relate policies, marketing and impacts to different types of running events and to outline how their dimensions shape certain actions, experiences and outcomes.

138 *Vassil Girginov*

The field of event studies has evolved considerably from its original concerns with operational and management aspects to more sophisticated and critical analyses of running events as social, cultural, political, environmental and economic phenomena. It has expanded its theoretical base by utilising a range of sociological, political and business theories such as event policy and politics (Foley et al., 2009), movement culture and geography (Bale & Sang, 2013; Qviström et al., 2020) and human rights (McGillivray & Duignan, 2022). A promising avenue for the future of running events studies has been Mair and Smith's (2021, p. 1741) suggestion that "rather than merely trying to understand how best to limit negative impacts, there is a need for research on the potential of events as tools for promoting, provoking and delivering sustainable development".

Running events and sustainable development

The growth of running events both as a field of scientific enquiry and as an industry has raised the question of their role in sustainable development. This question is closely intertwined with running policy, marketing and impacts, and is different from the question how to make running events sustainable. Half of the events studied in this book have been running for over ten years which illustrates their viability and sustainability. Nonetheless, even events that have been around for over 20 years are still facing serious challenges to their survival. The issue of events' sustainability concerns not only the competition with other events but a range of other important aspects that have gained prominence recently. These include the interactions of organisers and participants with nature, the use of environmentally sound management approaches, waste management, compliance with event industry sustainability standards (i.e., ISO20121 and sustainability sport event management standard) and others. These are complex issues that require careful planning, execution and resources.

Nonetheless, as Mair and Smith (2021, p. 1740) have argued, "we should no longer merely be trying to run 'sustainable events'; rather, we should focus on how events can contribute to the sustainable economic, social and environmental development of the places which host them". Such a paradigmatic shift requires first a political commitment on the part of public authorities and event organisers. This commitment should then be followed with practical actions, including promotion and delivery.

The political ground for the shift towards sustainable development was paved in 2017 by the adoption of UN Sustainable Development

Goals (SDG). Several major international sport organisations, including the International Olympic Committee and WA, have signed up to the SDG and put in place implementation strategies. Recently, climate change, as one dimension of sustainable development, has been in the political spotlight. Building on the impetus from the 2021 COP climate summit in Glasgow, nearly 300 international and national sport organisations have signed up to the UN Framework for Climate Action in Sport (https://unfccc.int/climate-action/sectoral-engagement/sports-for-climate-action). The framework requires organisations to pledge commitment to climate targets, to plan, proceed with action and report on their actions. This represents a strategic change in sport organisations' policy and operations with far-reaching political, social and economic consequences. The international governing body of athletics, WA, as one of the signatories to the UN Framework for Climate Action in Sport, has become the first organisation with a 10-year sustainability strategy (WA, 2020). Running events of all kinds will also have to reconsider their contribution to sustainable living and make a concerted effort to use the power of running to transform people's and communities' lives. Further research also needs to explore the socio-cultural and environmental impacts of running events along with a better understanding of the relationship between events and public policy agendas.

References

Alexandris, K., Theodorakis, N., Kaplanidou, K., & Papadimitriou, D. (2017). Event quality and loyalty among runners with different running involvement levels: The case of "The Alexander the Great" International Marathon. *International Journal of Event and Festival Management, 8*(3): 292–307, https://doi.org/10.1108/IJEFM-08-2016-0057

Bale, J., & Sang, J. (2013). *Kenyan running: Movement culture, geography and global change.* London: Routledge.

Botella-Carrubi, D., Curras Mostoles, R., & Escrivá-Beltrán, M. (2019). Penyagolosa Trails: From ancestral roads to sustainable ultra-trail race, between spirituality, nature, and sports. A case of study. *Sustainability, 11*(23): 6605.

Cairney, P. (2016). *The politics of evidence-based policy making.* New York: Springer.

CRAWFORD, A. (2021, NOV. 5). Exclusion to exclusivity: The history of women running the New York City Marathon. Available at https://www.si.com/edge/2021/11/05/history-women-running-new-york-city-marathon#:~:text=At%20the%20organization's%20annual%20convention, same%20race%20as%20the%20men

Edwards, B. & Gillham, P. (2013). Resource mobilization theory. In D. A. Snow, D. Della Porta, B. Klandermans, & D. McAdam (Eds.), *The Wiley-Blackwell encyclopedia of social and political movements* (pp. 1–6). Oxford: Blackwell Publishing.

Foley, M., McGillivray, D. & McPherson, G. (2015). Culturing sports mega events: leveraging public value. In: J. M. Bryson, B. C. Crosby and L. Bloomberg (Eds.), *Creating Public Value in Practice* (pp. 331–347). Boca Raton, FL: CRC Press/Taylor and Francis.

Gotham, K.F. (2005). Theorizing urban spectacles. *City, 9*: 225–246.

Handelman, D. (1990). *Models and mirrors: Towards an anthropology of public events*. New York: Bergham Books.

Herrick, C. (2015). Comparative urban research and mass participation running events: methodological reflections. *Qualitative Research, 15*(3), 296–313.

Mair, J., & Smith, A. (2021). Events and sustainability: Why making events more sustainable is not enough. *Journal of Sustainable Tourism, 29* (11–12), 1739–1755. DOI: 10.1080/09669582.2021.1942480.

Martin, J., & Hall, J. (2020). The impact of the New York City Marathon on hotel demand. *Economies, 8*(4): 89. https://doi.org/10.3390/economies8040089

McGillivray, D., & Duignan, M. B. (2022). Events, urban spaces and mobility. *Annals of Leisure Research, 25*(1): 1–4.

Peckover, S., Raineri, A., & Scanlan, A. T. (2022). An analysis of congestion during running events from the perspective of runners: Prevalence, impact on safety and satisfaction, and preferred controls. *Event Management, 26*(5): 967–978.

Qviström, M., Fridell, L., & Kärrholm, M. (2020). Differentiating the time-geography of recreational running. *Mobilities, 15*(4): 575–587.

Shipway, R., Holloway, I., & Jones, I. (2013). Organisations, practices, actors, and events: Exploring inside the distance running social world. *International Review for the Sociology of Sport, 48*(3): 259–276.

Snow, D., & Benford, R. (1988). Ideology, frame resonance and participant mobilization. *International Social Movements Research, 1*: 197–218.

WA (2020). *Sustainability Strategy 2020-2030*. https://www.worldathletics.org/download/download?filename=f779185b-65b0-46ab-af3b-1cd65a276f13.pdf&urlslug=Sustainability%20Strategy%202020-2030

Index

Note: **Bold** page numbers refer to tables; *Italic* page numbers refer to figures and page numbers followed by "n" denote endnotes.

Alexandris, K. 11, 19, 31, 33, 37, 50, 58, 61, 65–7, 71, 74–8, 92–3, 135
Association of Road Racing Statisticians (ARRS) 26,
athlete(s) 4, **10**, 20, **25**, 33, 74–5, 86, 136
athletics 4, 109, 111, 139; club 50, 58, 60; post-sport 20
authorities: local **13**, 36, 68–9, 95, 107–**8**, 110, 112, 135; public 19, 21, 39–40, 42, 107, 109–110, 133, 138

Balaska, P. 11, 92
brand 67, 76–9, 96, 103, 111, 129; associations 77; personality 77, 80; personality framework 77
branding 11, 73–4, 76, 78–80, 83, 102

case study: AG Antwerp Ten Miles & Marathon 11, **12**, 50, 51, *51*, 52, *52,* 53, **53**, 54, **55**, 56, 58, **106**, 111; Beijing Marathon 123, 127; Brussels 20km race 11, 50, 51, *51*, 52, 53, **53**, 54, **55**; Eindejaarscorrida Leuven 11, **12**, 42, 58–9, **106**, 111; LifeSouth Race Weekend 14, 79–80, 109, 111, 117–22, 136; Marathon Amersfoort 11, **13**, 65, 68–72, 81–2, 86–90, **107**, 111; Running Events in China 14, 101, 112, *123,* 123–130; The Athens Marathon: the authentic; 11, **12**, 65, 68–71, 77, 92–7

China's running boom 124, 136
city marathons 1, 21, 23, 27, 31, 39, 78, 88, 124, 127–130
civil society 19, *37*, 39, 42
class: middle-22, 34, 124–5; social 36, 73
club, 20, **25**, 34, 37–8, 42, 59–60, 63; athletic 20, 22, 33, 36, 37, *37*, 38, 39, 42, 50, 58, 60, 110; member 38, **106**; private 20; running **13**, 22, 50, 82, 90, 109, 111; sports 33, 38, 68–9, 110
co-creation 40, 69, 79, 88, 95
commercialisation 4, 22–4, 28, 38, 41, 50, 54, **100**, 132
commodification 6, 22–3, 38, 41
community 9, 40, 69, 74, 81, **101**–3, 105, 107, 109–110, 112, 117, 119–122, 133–4, 136; light **25**; running 36–**7**
comparison: cross-national 19, 33–4; cross-temporal 19, 26, 34
coopetition 63
corona virus 86–7
counterfactual use 102
COVID-19 24, 29, 51, *51*, 52, *52*, 66, 83, 92, 125–6, 129–30.
customer journey 56

Daring Club Leuven Atletiek **12**, 58, 63, 111
democratisation 22, **25**, 35, 41, 50, 54, 132

de-sportification 20, 41
de-traditionalisation 20, **25**, 33, 41
digitalisation 24, 28

economic impact 8, 42, 61, 65, 70–1, 75, 93, 99, 102, 119–120, 122, 126, 128–9, 132
event: auxiliary **10**, 54, 69–70, 88–9, 92–3, 95–6, 111, 128; concept 54, 62, 66, 68, 79, 82, 96, 135; course 60–1; identity 62; impact 6–7, 10–11, 58, 61–2, 65, 71, 83, 96, 98–100, **100**, 103–104, 106–109, 112, 121, 123, 129; interactions 103, 135; policy 6, 7, 14, 19, 58, 62, 83, 138; promoter 7, 10, 102–104, 107; public 5–8; scape 18–19, 23, 42; social impact 86, **101**–103, 120, 122, 124–5, 132; side **10**, 38, 60, 62, 69–70, 72, 137; stakeholders 54, 62, 63, 65, 68, 69, 70, 83, 95, 99, 107, 109–111, 124–5, 135–7; theme 23, 33, 38, 66, 78–80; type/typology 6–9, **10**, 67, 72, 76, 78, 100, 126–7; virtual *51*, 51–2, 126, 129–130; visions 10, 65, 71, 99, 104
events research 6, 100
events studies 6, 102, 138
experience: bodily 24, 36; economy 24; lived 24; social 54, 56, 71
extremisation 24, 41

festivalisation 24, 41
Flanders 29, *30,* 31, 34, *35*, 38, 50–1, 60
formal evaluation 9, 129
freedom 8, 18

Girginov, V. 1, 98, 109, 132
globalisation 23
Golazo Sports **12**, 58–61
government: local 22, *37*, 39, 58, 68–9, 87, 89, 124, 127–8 ; national 42, 125

Health: impact 93; mental 36, 74, 105; personal 23, 36; physical 2, 36; policies 21, 62; promotion 21
Helsen, K. 11, 18–9, 24, 29, *30*, 31, *32*, 33, 35, 37, 42n6, 50–1, 58, 62

Hover, P. 11, 20, 23, 28, 40, 65, 69–70, 86

impact: intangible 4, 86, 98, 102–3, **106–7**, 110, 112, 120–1, 135–6; tangible 4, 98, 102–3, 112, 122, 135; type(s) of 68, 83, 87–8, 93, **100**
individualisation 23
industry: running 19–20, 22–3, 36, 38–40, 126, 129–130; tourist 22
influencers 60
informalisation 20, 33, 41, 54
intentional development 104

jogger 20, **25**, 33, **37**, 74
jogging 3, 22

Kaplanidou, K. 71, 102, 117, 120
Karagiorgos, T. 11, 74, 92

leveraging 4, 69, 107–9, 111
lifestyle 5, 18, 36, 39, 59, 62–3, 63n1, 70, 76, 78, 89, 98, **101**–2, 107, 124, 136
Liu, Y. 11, 14, 123
logic model 101, 109
loneliness 18

marathon: ultramarathon 2, 24; World Marathon Majors 31, 124
marathoning 26, 28, 31–2
marketing 65–97; city 58–9; communication 11, 60, 67, 72–4, 76, 79–82, 89, 92, 96; destination 39, 70–1, 75, 77, 80, 128; digital 72, 81–3, 89; place 23, 65–6, 70–2, 75–7, 80, 87, 93, 103; promotion(al) 7, 14, 65–7, 69–73, 76, 80–82, 89, 96, 102, 112, 135–8; time 65–6, 71–2, 75, 77, 87, 93
market segmentation 56, 73, 77
media: coverage 71, 128–9; social 24, 60, 80–3, 110, 119–120, 124, 128, 130, 136
model: co-governance management 40; multi-governing 41; multi-sector *37*; tripartite governance 41
modes of running 2

National Running Tracker 2
neoliberal 18
Ntovoli, A. 11, 74, 92

Ooms, L. 11, 65, 69, 76, 86

physical endurance 18
pilgrimage 18
policy: actors 36, health 62; public 6, 11, 23, 112, 139; public welfare 21, 42
prize money 4, 87, 128
product: augmented product 67, 69, 72, 93, 96; core product 67, 70, 96; tangible product 67–8
product diversification 28
professionalisation 24
public value 14, 19, 39–42, 68–9, 79, 109–112, 136

race: marathon 26, 93, 118; obstacle 23; road 4, 28, *28*, *37*, 125–6, 130n1; running 24, 28, 31, 33, 72, 92
resource: development 108; event 107, **108**, 109; mobilisation 98, 109
responsibility 40, 107; social 40, 42, 93
revolution: cultural 20, **25**; fitness 20, 50; recreational 20
run: beach 33; city 2, 23, **25**, 33; colour 23, 33, 38, 79; desert 24; fell 2; ladies 32–3, 38, 50, *52*, *53*; mountain 24, 130n1; mud 23; obstacle 33; short 50, 52, *52*, *53*; start to 32, 38
runner(s): competitive 2–3, 54, 74, 110; marathon 18, 30, 96; non-competitive 38; recreational 3, 19, 21, 33, 37, 39, 54, 68, 92, 105, 134
runners: motivation 2–3; motives 74, 80; profiles 18–19, 31, 73; types of 2
running: boom 3, 18, 20, 123–4, 126, 130, 136 ; classifications 1, 7; functional role 1; injuries 3, 6, 130; (long-)distance 18, 20, 37; mass 3, 21, 36; manufactured 3, 4, 134; non-traditional 23, 42; quantified running self 24; recreational 2, 18, 21–3, **25**, 28–9, 33–6, *37*, 38–42, 69, 75, 86; sportscape 23; studies 5, 6; wave 20–1, 23–4, **25**, 26–7, 31–3, 41, 51

Scheerder, J. 2, 6, 11, 18–24, 26, *26*, 27, *27*, 28, *28*, *30*, **30**, 31, *32*, 33–34, *35*, 35, 36, 37, 38–9, 41, 50–1, *51*, *52*, 53, **53**, 54, *55*, 58, 78, 86
segmentation criteria 73
self-actualisation 18
self-discipline 18, 24, 36
self-monitoring 24
self-tracking 24
social capital 38, 102–3, 120, 122
social equality 23
social integration 21, 39–40
social welfare 103
socialisation 39
society 2, 6, 18, 39, 104, 109: civil 19, *37*, 39, 42
sponsor 60–1, 68–9, 87, 89, 92, 95, 108, 110, 112, 117, 128, 132; name 59; packages 59; title 61
sponsoring *37*
sponsorship 4, 61, **108**, 127,
Sport for All: movement 21; policy 21; programmes 42
standardisation 4, **25**, 135
status: social 19, 34, 36, 41, 75; social status pyramid 34, *35*; social status symbol 36; socio-professional 34, *35*
subsidiarity 39

target audience 65, 68–9, 73, 76, 80, 82, 88, 93
technology of the body 3–4
theory of change 101, 104
tourism 30, 65, 69, 71, 75, 93, 95, 100, **100**, **101**, 102, 112, 118–9, 122, 128–9
trail: run 2, 24, 33, 72, 126–7; urban 2, 23, 33
trend 11, 19, 24, **25**, 28–9, 42n4, 50, 53–4, 83, 112, 124; time-trend data 26; time-trend perspective 28; time trend statistics 34

virtualisation 24
volunteer *37*, 37, 38, 40, 60, 67, 71, 76, 93, 95, 102, **108**, 110, 120, 132

well-being 1, **10**, 76, 101–2, **106**, 112, 136; social 8, 68; mental 18, 68, 80
World Athletics 2, 4, 28, 31, 126, 134

For Product Safety Concerns and Information please contact our EU
representative GPSR@taylorandfrancis.com
Taylor & Francis Verlag GmbH, Kaufingerstraße 24, 80331 München, Germany

www.ingramcontent.com/pod-product-compliance
Lightning Source LLC
Chambersburg PA
CBHW051748230426
43670CB00012B/2201